# UNBOUND

## The Cycle Of Ascendancy

## How Your Life Evolves Around It

### DORIEN ISRAEL

*Edited by Donna Hepburn*

Note for Librarians: A cataloguing record for this book is available from Library and Archives Canada at www.collectionscanada.ca/amicus/index-e.html

ISBN 1-4120-6130-X

PUBLISHING™

*Offices in Canada, USA, Ireland and UK*
This book was published *on-demand* in cooperation with Trafford Publishing. On-demand publishing is a unique process and service of making a book available for retail sale to the public taking advantage of on-demand manufacturing and Internet marketing. On-demand publishing includes promotions, retail sales, manufacturing, order fulfilment, accounting and collecting royalties on behalf of the author.

**Book sales for North America and international:**
Trafford Publishing, 6E–2333 Government St.,
Victoria, BC v8t 4p4 CANADA
phone 250 383 6864 (toll-free 1 888 232 4444)
fax 250 383 6804; email to orders@trafford.com
**Book sales in Europe:**
Trafford Publishing (uk) Limited, 9 Park End Street, 2nd Floor
Oxford, UK ox1 1hh UNITED KINGDOM
phone 44 (0)1865 722 113 (local rate 0845 230 9601)
facsimile 44 (0)1865 722 868; info.uk@trafford.com
**Order online at:**
trafford.com/05-1031

10 9 8 7 6 5 4 3

This book is about you – your path, your journey, your process. Within Unbound you will experience an "energy" of high vibration that has the ability to shift perception. Because of this, these words can create miracles when you apply the principles to the unique situations and experiences in your life.

If you have picked up this book, that possibility is well on the way to becoming reality. You are already on a path of Ascendancy. Unbound comes only to those who are ready for a transformation, ready to make a transition to a higher level of understanding.

# How to Work This Book

This book, meant to be worked as well as read, seeks readers attempting to enhance their power to act on their own behalf, the self-healers to whom this book is dedicated.

These readings and exercises come together by careful design. The order of these readings is significant as you will see from the feelings and emotions released from each of the major sections of this book. There is energy in this workbook. Its powerful exercises on the focus pages that follow, can help you alter the view you hold of yourself -- the key to all other changes you wish to manifest in your life.

Your negative belief system limit the truth of who you are -- a whole, abundant, dynamic, empowered, creative, compassionate being. By expanding your beliefs you will be able to witness instantly changes in what you perceive as "reality."

The three major sections of this workbook, "Tradition, Transition, and Transformation," address the process you go through when you wish to allow growth or change into your life. The first section, "Tradition", attempts to help you acknowledge that what was once acceptable in your life may no longer serve you. The "Transition" writings strengthen your ability to search for alternative beliefs, ones that serve to uplift your spirit and sharpen your awareness. The "Transformation" readings and exercises prepare you to experience expansion and allowance.

This process, this Cycle of Ascendancy, shall be available to you again and again, whenever you seek to travel the path of self-discovery and experience anew the wonder of your divine spirit in human form. Your spirit, like all living things upon this plane, seeks to move and evolve because what does not move stagnates and becomes extinct.

This Cycle of Ascendancy forever feeds into itself, more a process than a destination. This workbook may be used whenever you feel you have stopped your forward motion and are holding on to the illusion of "safety" within Tradition. When you fear to experience the unexplored, it is time to work this book again.

There is a wise and wonderful teacher within you. Working this book will help you to call upon this wisdom. You will intuitively know what speed is best for you. Sometimes you will focus on a chapter for a week or more. At other times your attention will be needed perhaps for only a day. It is up to you, for it is truly your process.

Most reading are followed by exercises designed to help you implement and integrate the principles and concepts contained in the section you have just read. The readings will catch your attention and occupy your mind. The exercises speak to your heart and soul through the only language they understand -- experiential knowingness.

# TABLE OF CONTENTS

# Introduction

I'm not sure this book needs an introduction from me, since it's more about you; your path, your journey, your process. Within Unbound you will experience an energy of high vibration that has the ability to shift perception. Because of this I believe these words can create miracles when you apply the principles to the unique situations and experiences in your life.

What I have come to like and trust most about this information is that it seeks no guru and demands no allegiance. There is no church to build and no place to go to except within yourself. This material is not interested in supplanting or in any way overriding your own intuitive process. It does not dictate, direct or demand. It is not meant to compete with any belief system you already hold. It simply suggests the possibility of other paths open to you that can lead to higher spiritual ground.

These words have changed me, not so much because of my role in writing them down, but because like you I work this material. It has made a huge difference for the better in my life. I was not a spiritual person. As a natural extrovert, I looked outside myself for my happiness, approval, beliefs, and goals. I knew no other way to be but that all changed in 1984.

Driving home late one night after a business meeting I had a serious automobile accident. I was feeling depressed, thinking about how my life seemed to contain so little satisfaction and my work was such a struggle. Just before impact I remember thinking that this might be an easy way out. I slammed on the breaks, but too late. My next memory was of walking over to a police officer who was searching the woods off to the side of the road.

As I approached the officer, I said "What are you looking for"? He replied "I'm looking for the driver of this car." "I'm the driver of this car." I said. He looked up and somberly said "Oh, no lady, you couldn't be, the driver of this car is not standing."

Miraculously I was unhurt, though the driver's side of the car was mangled and crumpled. Stunned, I wondered how had I had managed to walk away?

Prior to the accident I knew that I needed to change my stressful life, but was too terrified to do it. For ten years I had been a successful real estate agent and had a good career that had been financially lucrative and personally fulfilling. Juggling a career, marriage and mothering, I believed I could "have it all." But I was having trouble keeping it all together and tried hard to deny the deep sense that something was not right, hoping it would go away, hoping change would not be necessary.

After the accident, I no longer had the will to hold on to all the pieces of my life and decided to quit my job. This meant we had to sell our home, change my daughter's school and give up the 'things' I had worked so hard to acquire. My husband threatened to leave me.

I was in a lot of pain and confusion. I knew I had to follow my deep intuitive feelings, but that path seemed to be causing my family so much heartache. Around this time a friend suggested that perhaps my dreams would help me decipher what was happening in my life. I put a pen and a pad of paper by my bed so I could capture my first waking thoughts.

On July 19, the day after my 37th birthday, I began to write what I assumed to be dream fragments but instead I received the first of what would be many hundreds of messages.

I wrote what I heard, *"Good morning! Happiness and joy are now yours! You have the power within, you must simply choose between yourself and the world. Wholeness is on the way. We are proud of your continued success and steps toward true freedom. We are forever with you."*

This was not reassuring news to me at the time. I felt that on top of all my other problems I was now hearing voices! Voices! Oh my God I really had gone crazy. I hid the pad under the bed and decided not to tell a soul. Maybe this stuff would go away. It didn't. Every morning it was there and every morning I wrote.

Slowly the writings began to change my perspective on life. The messages became clearer and I began to trust their wisdom and also the feelings the words carried with them. As I picked up the pen and paper I felt a sense of expansion flood over me . I began to hear very specific words. Many times the concepts were larger than the the words used to describe them and so there would be clarifying sensations or images allowing me to see beyond the limitation of the words I was writing.

Some weeks later, after my shock at being able to communicate with another dimension had worn off, I asked "Who am I talking to?". The reply was "...from a source you share with Christ consciousness". When I asked "Why me?" The reply was, "Why not you? You are not special, only open and willing."

The messages in time changed from a purely personal nature to a more public one. I was asked if I would trust enough to allow others to come and listen to these teachings. I wrote each day and then on Wednesday nights a group would gather in our house who wanted to hear what I had written. For the next three years this gathering met to meditate and work the material that has now been published as Unbound. I will be forever in the debt to that special group for their support and encouragement.

For many years after those gatherings ended, the material was "unbound" with copies of the individual readings simply made and handed from person to person. I don't know how far the material traveled in that loose form, but one day a few years ago, my

3

husband took his seat in an airplane looked over at the person sitting next to him and saw the Unbound readings, heavily underlined on ragged paper!

Unbound was privately published in Hong Kong and translated and published in Japan. The books have been passed around the world until there were no more left. Now, with some updating I am happy to have it made available again.

My hope for you is that you find and truly trust your own unique path. If Unbound is even a small stepping stone for you along your way, I have even more reason to give thanks for the blessings that have come to me this lifetime.

*Dorien Israel*

# A Gift

This is what I heard... and this is my Gift to you.

*We are gladdened to be within your Divine Presence.*
*It is indeed a present that we bring you*
*in the form of peace of mind,*
*a mind at rest in the Presence of God.*

*Where is the Presence of God?*
*Where do you need to go in order to find such a gift?*

*Everything for which you so diligently search*
*shall be found at the sacred sector between Self and Source,*
*two dimensions intersecting,*
*Heaven revealed through you, on earth.*

*Your success on this journey is assured*
*for you have always stood within this radiant Presence.*
*There is nowhere to go in order to find your happiness,*
*yet a shift in perception is mandatory to your success.*

*Regardless of how far away you might search,*
*only will you find yourself.*
*There is no way to distance yourself from this eternal connection,*
*instead you must only stop,*
*be silent and stay still*
*for everything to be revealed.*

You have cried out in loneliness and despair, begging in your
heart for the answers the mind cannot give, *"Who am I? Where is
God?"*

You know all things beloved, and yet insist on fragmenting and separating yourself from your own understanding.

*It is time to bind together through the heart,*
*that which has been separated by the mind,*
*so you might live forever within the unity of the spirit.*
*Answer the the question with the words that form it,*
*"God is who and where I  AM"*

*You are Bound by the unified creative force,*
*the movement behind all life, called by you as Source.*
*You are Bound by your commitment to the process called unfoldment.*
*You are Bound by an impeccable nature to fulfil your destiny on earth.*

*All these things shall you be Bound by,*
*but from this time on, you may choose to be forever Unbound*
*by all the restrictions and limitations that have, in the past,*
*encumbered your mind, your body, and your spirit.*

*It is your destiny this lifetime to be*
*Unbound in your quest toward realization.*
*Let it come to pass now.*

# Stages Of Life

*"In order to move more toward the light,*
*you must first be willing to step out in*
*faith through the darkness. Darkness is all*
*that remains after the light of experience*
*has been consumed by the soul through*
*the process of discovery."*

In order to become Unbound, you need only transcend the mundane and ordinary view you hold both of self and the life you are living. Alter the perception of your purpose on this planet, and you will automatically transform its nature and character. Change is found only through your willingness to perceive your own purpose differently. Expand your beliefs and you shall expand your experience.

Your power to change reality is supreme. You are all master alchemists in your ability to transform your lives. There is a great vision held within you. It is your quest this lifetime to remember, reclaim, and rejoice in it. It is the perceptions of the mind that constrict the range and depth of that vision. Your eyes are blinded by beliefs that no longer serve you. Without true sight you see only external limitations rather than your own inner vastness.

So it shall be the purpose of this teaching to become Unbound. Together we shall identify and isolate your fears, doubts, and despair so you might become unbound through a powerful process called recognition. We shall present you with the opportunity to overcome these limitations so that you might free yourself from paralysis and overcome your greatest fear – change.

Separation appears to be a reality upon this plane, a false perception creating only anguish. No longer see those things that share your world as separate or apart from you. Instead, see that you are miraculously bound together by the causative factor of light and movement – synonymous with life and love. Known by many names on your planet, its sole purpose is to be recognized by you.

Life as experienced by many upon this plane is one dimensional with no space for expansion. Life appears to them as stagnant, or at best a linear progression with a definite beginning and an end. We ask that you alter your perceptions, so you might expand your experience.

Perceive life as a myriad of spirals, spheres, and cycles, unending in its progress. Your world is formed from endless cycles which cause the rotation of your solar system, the four seasons of your year, the movement of your tides, the waxing and waning of your moon, the ingressing and egressing of your soul. These cycles are responsible for life's eternal renewal and restoration.

To understand these cycles, to acknowledge their progression and respect their nature shall make you powerful. To ignore their message is to be in constant pain and confusion concerning your own nature and process.

You may learn much from these cycles of nature, yet they are constant and unchanging with little or no ability to progress. Only you, beloved, are engaged in a cycle that is dynamic in nature and unending in evolution and it is your destiny to travel upon her – the Cycle of Ascendancy.

The Cycle of Ascendancy is a cycle of completion within a crystalline spiral. This cycle, unlike any other, is one of growth, of change, of unfoldment and greater knowledge of all aspects of self including those known as masculine and those known as feminine. All cycles which exist upon this plane are feminine in nature. All who are willing to surrender to their feminine wisdom shall find themselves upon a journey within that is graceful and gentle.

The Cycle of Ascendancy is the other side of the masculine view of the world as constricting and limited to beginnings and endings, to straight lines and angles too narrow for rites of passage. Those who attempt to be delivered into a new realization by this point of view shall find themselves laboring under the burden called serious misconceptions.

The Cycle of Ascendancy welcomes change. The major goal of masculine energy is to manipulate and maneuver the outer environment so as to cause as little true movement as possible. Movement, flow, natural evolvement or progression of events is seen as a threat to established order. When feminine energy is expressed you experience movement; when you act on your masculine energy you produce meaningless motion.

Movement indicates life: no movement, no life. Movement is divine in its nature and purpose. It is from divine movement that things shift, turn, change. Movement takes what is known and explored and arranges it into a different pattern. It is this altered design that appears dangerous to the mind. Movement will forever produce discomfort for the ego. Movement is always initiated by the deep self in its attempt to bring you more into an altered state of consciousness, or what you call enlightenment. Altered is not better nor worse, beloved, it is only constantly different.

Do not be deceived; you do not only move toward what has been called the "light" after death. What you call your life, beloved, is only a perpetual state of movement attempting to merge itself once again with the light source from which it originated. You are eternally moving toward that light, and your attempts to struggle

9

or resist only cause you discomfort. Relax; you are only trying to go home.

So then we shall speak of Tradition as the first stage in the Cycle of Ascendancy. Tradition is that state in which all things are understood, comprehended, and complete. It is here that familiarity is considered more important than fulfillment. The stage of Tradition has definite prescribed agreements and concrete boundaries which allow less and less flexibility as time goes on.

It is both the hope and the fear of those who stay in Tradition that it will continue forever without disruption. Some stay in Tradition long enough to learn how to link with the light, then transit easily, moving consciously in the direction of their greatest fears. Others stay in Tradition for years, denying what their heart has heard, waiting for external events to change their minds rather than risk any movement from within. Some even choose death as a means of movement only to find themselves reentering another lifetime at the exact point where they exited.

There is no way out, only through. It is only through your willingness to move, to grow, to change, that you shall find the way for you. You cannot wait for events or others to change so you might be given permission to move. The first step must be through your own intention. From this movement will all things be altered ultimately in your favor. This we promise.

All upon this plane have fears. For in all the cosmos, this is where you incarnate so that you might confront illusion. Yet it is exactly those illusions that will lead you toward the light in which shines all the peace, joy, fulfillment, protection, and love for which you long. When you insist you know not what to do, when you know not where to go – simply move toward your fears. For in this direction shall mastery be found.

What you seek is a process of confrontation, not a final destination. In order to move more toward the light, beloved, you must be willing to step out in faith through the darkness. Darkness is all that remains after the light of experience has been consumed by the soul through the process of discovery.

We have spoken of movement as that which nourishes the physical body, yet know that the spirit is nourished through the available light found in each new experience upon your path. The soul consumes this light in its attempts to merge with it. It is from this consumption of light that conscious expansion occurs.

It is your reluctance to move that keeps you within the darkness that houses despair, depression, doubt, and disease. Life is progressive and as such is in constant movement. As long as you are alive you must never stop moving, for movement is your consciousness attempting to become one with the light each new situation offers you.

Tradition, with its dimming light, becomes restrictive and barren. It is always the spirit, rather than the mind, that indicates the necessity for transit. The ego refuses to leave this security and so convinces you of danger beyond. At this sector you find yourself at a point of choice: to listen to the mind that speaks to you with fears, logic, and justifications or to the spirit which seeks freedom and fulfillment.

To stay too long in this now barren landscape called Tradition is to invite disease, depression, and certain death into your experience. Consciousness, as expressed on this plane of polarities, strengthens your ability to recognize available options and your courage to choose one option over another. Often you complicate the process of choice with all manner of irrelevant information supplied to you by the mind. Remember, the mind may be at direct odds with the spirit. It is in the heart and not the mind where you will find the insight you seek.

It is our intention to make this procedure called choice as simple as possible. It is most certainly simple. It is not, however, always easy.

11

Whenever you are presented with choice, choose life over death, light over darkness, and movement over stagnation. Transition is the process that facilitates movement from one choice to another.

So it is Transition that is the second stage in the Cycle of Ascendancy. Transition is the interim step taken along the path toward Transformation. Transition is a step out in faith. It is a trusting, a letting go. It is Transition that moves you into a state of receptivity and expectancy so that you are in a position to be filled with what is to come.

You live more closely to the curve of the circle and farther away from the security of the line while in the state of Transition. It is at this stage that you are closest to God, for you have momentarily abandoned all that you have been for the promise of what you might become. This is who we know God to be, a totally evolving consciousness, complete and whole at every moment, yet eternally expanding and unfolding.

To be in transit is to be within the movement of that Divine presence. Transition is a time rather than a place – a time for endings and beginnings. Transition leads you away from the traditional and into the transformational. It is a time to prepare for what is and what is to come and to be grateful for all that has been.

If your movement from Tradition is done willingly, your experience in Transition will be an exciting adventure enveloped by your sense of freedom. If on the other hand, you have stayed too long in Tradition and so caused external events to conspire against you in order to create the necessity of transit through trauma, then you will experience this time as crisis.

Often in this stage it will appear that there has been loss or failure. Know that this is an impossible illusion perpetrated by a devious mind that fears for its safety and wishes to keep you from ultimately experiencing your own.

Transition may be made smoothly and easily, or it may be felt as a wrenching away of everything you have held sacred and dear. Again, it is all in your perception. A transition made consciously will be characterized by a sense of relief from that which had become too confining and limiting. It may be felt as the jump into the void or seen as a leap of faith.

As you begin to free fall during this time of Transition you are more open, more receptive, more available, aware, expectant, and vulnerable. Though the sensation is one of falling, you actually ascend to a new level of consciousness.

Finally, your spirit will arrive at the brink of a new understanding ready to drink in the light of learning. It is at this new level of awareness where the final process in the Cycle of Ascendancy occurs – and so Transformation begins.

It is in this new realm of Transformation that you will begin to test and explore your own creativity. You will quite literally search for new opportunities to express who you are becoming. Those who have watched your courage may or may not follow your lead. Always will you find that this new domain supports life. Your doubts will be seen as unfounded.

In Transformation you will begin to incorporate new levels of consciousness within yourself. You have a keen sense of aliveness and are filled with gratitude for being delivered safely. Your gratitude binds you within the presence of God.

Transformation for a time will provide you with perfect balance and alignment. It is a place that holds optimum value for all of you. However, it is also within your expanded awareness that you will enthusiastically begin to build the very structure that in time will necessitate again your transiting.

Transformation, once loved by the spirit and feared by the mind, will eventually become constrictive to the spirit and supportive of the mind. It is then a place of limitation without light. Once again it is time to move.

You have been within this Cycle of Ascendancy from the moment of your very inception as sperm and egg. The womb first appeared to that original you as the grandest, most vast environment possible. Beyond comprehension was the possibility that this could ever become confining. Yet, as you continue through life to gather more and more of who you are becoming out of who you have been, you find you need to expand into even larger dimensions.

From your very beginning it has always been the discomfort you feel from confinement and limitation that pushes you forward into more and more life. This Cycle of Ascendancy causes the wheel of life to move and evolve. Those who refuse shall be removed. Those who are removed repeatedly shall become extinct and their consciousness will no longer be allowed to return to this planet.

Christ said *"become as the little children."* It is children who most easily move through these three stages: learning as quickly as possible, so they might progress; leaving easily what is already mastered for what is still mysterious; moving gracefully from Tradition, into Transition, and onto Transformation which must by the nature of consciousness become Tradition again – endless movement in each expanding moment, the finite giving way to the infinite.

We ask that you become consciously familiar with these stages so that you will recognize the signals that indicate desire for movement. Learn that struggle causes painful consequences and that you need not resist. Surrender to your love of life through your desire to move toward the light.

Trust that you cannot fall too far, for you already exist within the body of God, firmly held by this presence. You and God are companions who share a common destination – home. Welcome, to those who travel the Cycle of Ascendancy.

# CYCLE OF ASCENDANCY

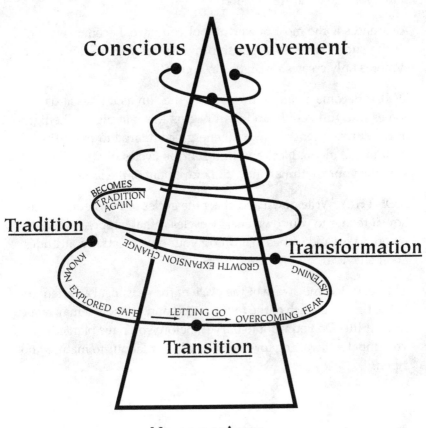

Conscious evolvement

Tradition

Transformation

BECOMES TRADITION AGAIN

GROWTH EXPANSION CHANGE

KNOWN EXPLORED SAFE

LISTENING

LETTING GO

OVERCOMING FEAR

Transition

Unconscious

# Focus on The Cycle of Ascendancy

All things upon this plane have a cycle. The power of these cycles influence your unique rhythms. The more sensitive you are to the movement found within nature, the more will you understand your own nature.

Awareness is the most powerful tool you have. Become aware of all the subtle signs that nature provides for you. To deny these symbols only creates resistance in your life.

DAILY: Become aware of the cycle of the sun as it rises at dawn, comes into full zenith, and then begins to set at night. The light of the sun is intense, powerful energy compared to the diffused light of the moon. Notice within self the cycles of your day and see how your rhythms follow the movement of the light.

MONTHLY: Write down and chart the cycles of the moon and see how it relates to your own energy cycles. What happens when the moon waxes and wanes in terms of your own creativity, attitudes, and behaviour?

YEARLY: Become aware of the cycle of the seasons. Pay attention to the timing of each of the four seasons and see how it may relate in your life. Do you want to harvest before you have planted? Are you impatient waiting for the fruits of your labour to mature and ripen?

# TRADITION

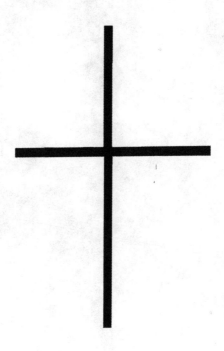

# Words

*"True communication is done with the heart; all else is noise made to make your mind feel as if you are not alone in this world of illusion."*

This book of words begins by saying there is too much talking, too little listening, too many words, and too little said. True communication is done with the heart; all else is noise made to make your mind feel as if you are not alone in this world of illusion. There is a great need for an economy of words, both between you and other and within your own mind.

Words come easily to those on the earth plane. You have turned talking into a desperate search for true meaning, but there is no meaning in words, only perception. You place much of your attention on looking for appropriate words.

You believe that if only the right words could be found then truth might be known and so communicated in a way that other would abandon his or her position and take up yours. Never with words alone will this shift occur.

It is a futile, energy-consuming game that costs the earth plane much, for you attempt to back up your words with force and too often with your lives and those of others. Your wars, both personal and among countries, are over the emotions and fears born of misgivings from the unsatisfying exchange of words between self and other. You use your words as weapons to attack or as

19

shields to defend yourself from the onslaught of verbal abuse – it is a game of fools and no one wins.

It is time for fewer words, not more. It is in the moment when no words are spoken that truth is most available to you. When you are engaged in the act of passion, when you are in meditation, when you are at rest. These are the times when you are closest to expressing the only thing that needs communication – love; love of self, love of other, love of God.

Words are necessary, but the simpler the message the more accurate the meaning, the more precise the understanding. From all things that are real come truth, even without speech. The earth, the sky, the sea, the air, the babe that suckles, and the child that sleeps speak to you without words and your soul has no difficulty interpreting their message. Attempt to dissuade others from their point of view no longer through your words, for they truly cannot understand your language. Allow others to have their own direction and you take yours, trusting that you both will meet at a place destined to bring you together in a more meaningful way.

Walk your path, and allow others to walk their way. Know that all paths are sanctioned by God, that in reality it is God who has chosen to walk both paths to experience each. In giving this freedom, you lose the need for constant approval of others and the unforgiving urge to correct and judge. In giving this freedom, you set yourself and others free from lonely, unsatisfying attempts to nurture your spirit with words and you begin to listen instead to the small still voice within you.

If you understood the power of the spoken word uttered in anger, none of you would use it in the abasement of each other, self, the earth, or God. Your spoken words are invisible and because you cannot touch, smell, hear, or taste them, you believe they have no force or energy. These are primitive criteria and there is much truth and beauty existing beyond their reach. The guns, the arsenals, the wars, your personal defenses, no matter how sophisticated or deadly you believe them to be, are as a NO THING when compared to the power contained in one word expressing as the open heart.

In the beginning there was the word and the word was with God and the word was "good." Literally, the word was "good," pronounced and declared throughout the universe. The word, the thought, the command, the expression, came from the first Source and it was spoken as the word "good."

Go today and say less with your words and more with your eyes, with your heart, with your gestures, with your intentions. Know that the only word the soul can hear is the word "good," and that all other words are meaningless or do damage to your body.

"Good, Good, Good" – say these words to self and all you meet today and see the release in their eyes, for there will be a remembrance of that word from the inception of creation resounding through the cosmos. "It is good."

# Focus on Words

For a number of days (you set the duration) refrain from reading the newspaper, listening to television or radio news. Do not allow the mind to insist that you must be informed. Instead listen to your inner voice that is often drowned out from the commotion of external sound. Give yourself an opportunity to hear the words spoken within.

Upon arising each morning for 10 minutes become aware of how wonderful everything in your life really is. Allow your eye to fall easily on all things that make up your surroundings. As you look at the most ordinary and mundane objects, mentally vibrate the word "good." Begin to balance what the world says is information with what your heart says is truth. You will begin to have a remembrance of a time in your life when everything truly was good – and so see with a new perception.

# Expectations

*"Many of you would fall to your knees
in utter despair if you knew how many
times in the past you have thrown away
miracles simply because they did not
meet with the descriptions set by your
expectations."*

Expectations represent the guidelines set by the ego for unhappiness and disappointment. Your expectations allow the past to judge and limit your future. It is our wish that those beauteous souls reading this teaching participate fully in what is occurring on this page and within self at this perfect moment, free of the intrusion of expectation.

Each of you has thoughts of what shall be considered as useful experience. These expectations have their origin in the moment, but they inevitably draw you toward a future you judge, again and again, to be imperfect.

Expectations hold within them the promise of a "perfect future" as seen through the veil of limited judgment. They represent the ego's attempt to make you miserable by setting up and controlling your reaction to the always unfinished, expanding, and creative future that is given to you moment by moment.

Expectations remove you from the eternal now, taking you to a place of fantasy where what you hope will transpire clouds your perception of what is. You miss the moment in which you are engaged, beloved, as you begin to set up, through the limitation of expectations, your own future disappointment.

You are then disappointed because the definition prescribed by the ego of what the future must look like if it is to be satisfying cannot be found. Should the future fail to appear to meet this description, as proposed by the limited mind, it will then convince you of your inalienable right to experience discouragement. From this discouragement you find justification to draw conclusions concerning the acceptability of life and your role therein.

To be free of expectations and yet truly expectant is to be free of the need to control and limit the situations in which you find yourself. It is a great gift to be expectant and so remain aware of the magnificence unfolding in the perfection of each moment.

Do you believe that the expansive future you seek can come from a fantasy of expectations created by the mind in the present? Do you seriously believe that these limitations projected onto the vastness of the future will result in anything other than your own frustration and unhappiness?

Using the limited criteria of expectation to judge future moments places you off balance. The danger is that you miss much of what each moment has to offer because of the mind's expectation of what that moment should look like. The mind has, once again, set up a perfect way for you to fail. You are forever unaware of the constant beauty found by living life moment by moment as instead you pull dead expectations forward into the enlivened moment.

By locking yourself into the prison of expectation, you often miss the very thing for which you so desperately search. The reason you cannot find that which you seek is that you do not recognize it from the limited description set by your expectations.

You on the earth plane are engaged in a series of what might be called "treasure hunts." Upon each incarnation your inner being,

24

your God self, decides upon a list of things that are to be discovered during the life experience. Do not allow the ego mind to characterize those items on the intuitive list.

How does your mind believe peace looks? What of prosperity, friendship, happiness, and enlightenment? Your expectations have rigidly defined all these states of being and should you come across what does not fit the description you discard it. Many of you would fall to your knees in utter despair if you knew how many times in the past you have thrown away miracles simply because they did not meet with the descriptions set by your expectations.

How much more exciting to bring the expectancy of ongoing aliveness and sense of wonder into your future. To expect to be happy without setting perimeters. To expect to be prosperous and allowing for all the possible forms that might take. To expect to have friendship regardless of what face your friend might show you. To expect to be loved without limiting it by whom or in what way. To expect to know God in whatever way most appropriate for you at any moment of your life.

Forever receptive within the unfolding moment, opening to all it contains for you. When you are jubilantly in the state of expectancy rather than limited by specific expectations set in the past, your awareness is heightened from being open to all the possibilities contained within each moment.

This heightened state of living adds to and blends with the consciousness of the moment, rather than separating and removing you from it. The excitement of anticipation you feel is natural, for it is your intuition, your inner knowingness telling you how magnificent it is to experience the undefined moment.

Understand that you have the power to choose between creating a future built upon your conscious commitment to the moment or a future that rests upon limited expectations shaped by the past.

25

This choice provides you with the opportunity to project responsibly and consciously into the future.

Go today and know that what you seek can never be found within the confines of the expectations set forth by the limited ego mind. No longer attempt to project this narrow view given by the ego onto the expansive future. By so doing you will forever lose your disappointment in not finding value and joy in each moment of your life, moments that too often pass unnoticed in the darkness brought by expectation.

# Focus on Expectation

Nothing ever happens outside of the precious moment. The more you stay conscious within each moment, the more you will receive valuable information for future decisions.

Practice being in the moment. The here and now is all you have in order to effect a better future. Pull your consciousness back into your body and pay attention to her.

Is there tightness or discomfort? Look around at your immediate space. Notice the colors, listen carefully for any sounds. Close your eyes and listen to internal sounds, try to see the colors that dance on the backs of your eyelids, then finish by asking yourself "Where am I?" then answer "I am here." Ask "What time is it?" Answer "Now."

Reflect on the possibility that everything in the future is dependent upon your being conscious within the present moment. The more you can live in the here and now the more energy will be available for you to make the decisions that will manifest a better future.

# Beliefs

*"Your power is profound, so complete,*
*so absolute that you may even use it to*
*pretend you are not a god, the ultimate*
*limitation of a belief."*

Energy follows your thoughts out into the physical world, but your beliefs serve as the mortar of your experience.

Beliefs shaped by the ego mind will attempt to convince you that separation, hostility, and despair are real. Your ego has convinced you that these beliefs are accurate reflections of the world in which you live. The mind holds that these beliefs are based on objective, factual reality and then projects this view of the past into the future, giving you only the illusion of a present.

It is madness for you to hold any belief that is contrary to the truth of who you be. It is madness for you to allow your choices to be limited by the petty tyranny of the mind. It is madness if you refuse to acknowledge your own power in constructing your reality. It is madness that a powerful god should feel threatened by illusions you yourself have created.

Know that there exists no objective reality outside of self. External events, although they may appear to be separate from you, are in fact only products of your own creative nature. You have created every experience in your life through a system of cause and effect and it has all been for the purposeful good of instruction.

Yet because you refuse to assume responsibility for your experiences your lives are confusing and chaotic. You are the creators of your own reality, and you are fully accountable for what you experience within it.

If you do not like your experiences, change the thoughts and beliefs that are responsible for their conception. To alter any event in your external reality, you must first identify the internal belief that creates that experience.

Confront and directly challenge all beliefs, assumptions, judgments, and prejudices. If you find they support an uplifted view of who you are, keep them. If they limit and constrict your glory, discard them.

Do not be confused; regardless of whether you discover your beliefs to be supportive or destructive, they are not you. A belief is only a tool your being uses to embrace or negate life. Even your most expansive belief can become a limitation to your growth. You are unlimited and have no need of beliefs that keep you heavy and dense. As you become more willing to challenge your beliefs and form new ones that enhance your growth, you will literally grow lighter and cast a brilliant radiance.

The great masters on your plane who have achieved ascension have done so through discarding negative beliefs. Like them, you need go nowhere in order to reach heaven. Your heaven and your hell are created by your beliefs and it is solely your choice as to where you shall reside.

To witness the power of your own beliefs simply look at the difference between who we know you to be – a powerful, capable, compassionate, trusting, whole, committed, abundant, joyful, loving being – and how you are expressing in your life. If these were your beliefs about yourself, your entire universe would transform instantly.

Instead you prefer to listen to the ego mind telling you this is arrogance, and that you are undeserving of such consideration. Remember, the world will always show you an accurate view of your current beliefs. It is fully your choice as to what you believe and in this realization shall be found your greatest tool for freedom – free will.

A belief may either deny you your identity or fulfill you; it is your choice. Some beliefs hold a higher vibration than others and may help you discover your truth. No longer deny yourself the light for which you search; see the light within and simply choose a belief that allows more of your power and wonder to express.

To the extent that you are willing to confront your own beliefs you will facilitate your process in the Cycle of Ascendancy. Before you make a physical move you must alter the belief responsible for keeping you bound. If you persist in denying your own culpability in its creation, you will resist any movement toward expanding your beliefs, toward assisting you in your journey out of Tradition through Transition and into Transformation.

Your power is so profound, so complete, so absolute that you may even use it to pretend you are not a god, the ultimate limitation of a belief.

In the beginning, before time as you count it, there was the Infinite Source who loved itself well and from this love began to expand so that the Source might come to know more of its own perfection. An opportunity was created for the parts of the wholeness to perceive themselves as separate in order to experience the beauty of their own uniqueness. This experience of uniqueness is called individual consciousness and all who come to express upon this plane are engaged in it. It has been the grandest of adventures for the most courageous of souls.

Yet there was created simultaneously within that memory the fear of abandonment which supports your fear of unworthiness and all other fears on this plane. The fears that you were wrong and could be abandoned created a sense of lack within your being called unworthiness that manifests in your life as self-denial. You believe yourself unworthy of the riches of heaven and so you have created your version of hell within your own life and in the collective life you share with all existence on the earth plane. You have divided into various groups that share negative, limiting beliefs, groups that threaten the very planet that supports all life. You have built powerful weapons to defend your belief of separation and abandonment.

How might we convince you that this is not how the Source, known as God, views the purpose of the exploration known as life? You are living parts of the whole that is grateful for your willingness to go forth and express individual godness. Yet you neither feel nor return this gratitude, doubting instead your very reason for being.

Because you doubt yourselves, there is a lacking in your being, an insufficiency in your soul. The mind has told you that you are in need of a disguise, for you are not enough. This disguise is called your image and it is based on the belief of lack. This image keeps you from receiving what you truly want, from being recognized by those who have incarnated this lifetime in order to know you. They have a message of gratitude from God yet cannot find you under the image you project.

Under that image, constructed from your beliefs, assumptions, prejudices, and opinions, hides your godness: an endless source of light, an unbound spirit, a channel of divine consciousness, eternally connected to all living things as well as to the unified source from which it has all sprung. What belief, beloved, is worth projecting any other image? What belief would serve you as well?

The ego will insist that your image, your beliefs, your values, are who you are, that to abandon any one of them is to annihilate a part of self. Yet it is precisely this type of loss that shall deliver you to a fearless life. You must be willing to kill off the beliefs of the ego if you wish to live the life of the spirit.

You who read these words are ready to cast off such beliefs, to drop the mask, to risk and to expose self to self and to the world, to become Unbound.

You have been given a great gift to help win your freedom. Where would you imagine this gift to be, how far would you travel, how much would you pay for that which might release you from your limiting beliefs?

You have never been separated from this gift, yet you have not always recognized its value. In the past the ego mind has kept this tool from your discovery, using it for its own devious purposes. It is now time for you to reclaim the original intention of this gift.

There exists within your vast consciousness, beloved, a system which has the ability to encourage and promote even more consciousness. When it is used in accordance with its intended purposes it shall grant you the treasures of your universe. It is as yet not fully understood by your scientists but it is known by them as Reticular Activating System (RAS).

As now used by the ego mind, RAS functions as a powerful line of defense against those external images called your experiences which might conflict with a currently held belief. It acts as a screening or monitoring device that allows into your awareness only select sensory impressions (electromagnetic impulses) and blocks others. It is through this system that certain things are attracted to your attention and others are ignored.

This system of admittance into your awareness is initiated and activated through your beliefs. RAS only allows into your awareness those events which support your beliefs. So it can be a vicious cycle. You only notice what you already believe to be there and you only receive what you believe you may have. What you see is what you believe.

This once valuable gift has become for many a system of limitation and confinement. Used in this restrictive way it serves only to protect and promote the fears in the ego mind. By allowing only those situations into your awareness that support the mind's preconceptions, it has the ability to shape your sense of reality.

In truth. this mechanism was given to you as a means of total expansion and unlimited growth. For you only have to request more peace, more understanding, more abundance, more joy and love and it must by Law focus on those things which will deliver that experience to you. But in the past your RAS system has been a miracle misused.

Expand your beliefs and you will be able to alter the directional focus of your RAS so that it will be able to help you to locate all the endless possibilities that correspond to your new belief. Begin this process by believing that there exists no reality outside of self. Give up the delusion that even one solitary event might be experienced and understood exactly the same way by another.

There is no cold hard objective reality in your world as your mind would have you believe. There is only perception. You have come to experience this plane as an individualized consciousness, unique in purpose as well as perception. Listen to that still small voice, beloved, for it will speak to you of happiness and guide you to your own unique fulfillment.

Your unguarded words, expectations born of the past, and unchallenged beliefs create the collective confusion called by you as reality. If you are unhappy with the results it brings into your world, look to the beliefs that support and maintain them.

Listen carefully to your words, for contained within them are the messages that call forth your experience. Pay attention to your expectations. They are the promoters of unending unhappiness. Question your beliefs. They are the basis of your discontent and powerful tools for change.

33

You are a temporary traveler upon this path of physical realization. You retain the God-given ability to alter external realities through internal intentions. Change expectations which limit the expansive future by pulling you out of the glorious moment; use your positive intentions to project consciously a faultless future. Be open and vulnerable within your being, expressing your highest good, knowing that you can only hurt and be hurt by self.

To become more aware of your own beliefs, simply look at the results they create in your life. What internal assumptions support your physical "reality"? There is only one thing you may safely assume in life – your responsibility for creating it all. It is from this new awareness that you will then be given access, through your RAS, to those specific beliefs which have denied your vision.

You have the power to be still and to create the opportunity TO KNOW WHAT YOU KNOW, TO BE WHO YOU ARE, AND TO HAVE WHAT YOU WANT. It is time to listen to that part of self that has retained this vision and to approach your own destiny with an expanded belief in your honor and integrity.

## *Focus on Beliefs*

Beliefs that work support your desires; beliefs that don't, conflict. When a belief is in conflict with a desired result your experience will be one of struggle and frustration.

What you want but do not have in your life is due to your inability to manifest it based on a limited belief. It is essential that you become aware of your beliefs so that you might be free to change them when they no longer work.

Look at your beliefs about longevity, health and aging, disease, relationships. One way to witness your own beliefs is to write down assumptions or supposed facts. Your personal beliefs are often based on external information. For instance, if one out of every two marriages ends in divorce you may have formulated a personal belief that says "Why bother getting married? I've only got a 50/50 chance at making it work."

You may want to lose weight, but your underlying belief says "I have tried this hundreds of times and it's never worked so why would it this time?"

Once you have an awareness concerning a certain belief you can change it through affirmation. An affirmation is a positive intention toward a future goal. It is a positive written declaration in the present tense.

The mind believes what it is told with conviction and repetition. To change a currently held belief formulate a positive declarative sentence in present tense and write it 10 times before retiring and upon awaking for at least 21 days. I believe in this process and so the results are miraculous. What is your belief about what you have just read?

# Fear

*"You can never escape your fears by*
*running, for you have not legs fast*
*enough to outdistance an illusion."*

We have spoken of the Cycle of Ascendancy – a journey which allows for movement within the being as well as within the outward world. Yet you are free to choose a different route for there also exists an opposing cycle – the cycle of dependency. To follow this negative cycle is to become lost within Tradition through the illusion of fear, depression, and despondency and to become disoriented and confused. This cycle originates out of your fear to move, to surrender, to love. When you choose fear in any form you initiate pain, anger, depression, and guilt in your life. Your mind's addiction to the safe, the secure, and the known causes you to be fearful and to choose to travel within this cycle of dependency.

You always have choices and they are less complex than the mind would have you believe. Follow all emotions to their source and you will find only love or fear. It is always a simple matter to choose one over the other. Within your being you know that to choose love leads you toward the light. To choose love automatically unlearns fear, a most destructive emotion upon the plane of earth. To many of you fear, the largest illusion, is known as "truth." Fear is the first principle in the world of illusion and disease.

The feeling of fear relates to depression within the human soul. Fear, when unexpressed and ignored, causes a lack of self-esteem felt within the body as depression.

When you feed your fears through your attempts to avoid or ignore them, they grow. To deny your fears is to be ignorant of their nature and to become a victim of their illusion. Ignorance is the subtle combination of fear of the unknown mixed with hatred for what is not understood. In the beginning there was the first source and it knew and received itself well. It experienced no fear, knew no hatred, and was ignorant of nothing.

The source loved, understood, and knew itself and all of its parts of which you are one. The illusion of fear was created through a single thought – that separation from the divine was possible. The instant this thought occurred it was healed. Yet you continue to choose to experience the illusion of separation rather than surrender to the truth of unity.

In your world of contradictions and extremes you are allowed outrageous choices. These choices may lift you to the most exalted heights or they may plunge you into the depths of depression. Always are they your choices. Free will you call it. Within your mind, beloved, rests your heaven or your hell and it is through your choices that you add to either landscape daily.

Fear is a most desolate, dry, and tortuous way to view your world. Fear is not real, but the only way to experience this is to confront it. Fear, like any bully, simply grows arrogant of its strength when ignored. You actually increase its power through avoidance.

Fear has NO POWER itself, only the power you give it by non confrontation.

You feed your fears daily by not facing them and by creating expectations of what will happen when your fears are realized. You can never escape your fears by running, for you have not legs fast enough to outdistance an illusion. Your illusions shall follow you into the deepest recesses of your being, into other dimensions, and even unto death.

Many of you have in your past lives attempted to run from your fears through the peace thought to be found in death. How amusing, beloved, attempting to escape one illusion through the use of another you call death. After "death" you still must face those same fears, but you now have no physical vehicle to do so. All you lose in death is your body. All emotions, memories, and fears remain intact. So you incarnate again for the purpose of seeing through the illusion of fear.

Avoidance and denial shall be impossible when dealing with your FEARS. You have all been guilty of attempting to disown your own fears through projection onto the outer world as well as onto one another.

When you refuse to confront your individual fears, you sacrifice your own self-esteem, your dreams of peace, your impeccability, your integrity – your connection to the Source.

The lessons you wish to learn are all very literal. Lessons on this plane shall be easy to see if you stay awake and aware. You will forever lose valuable insight into your own destiny if you refuse to acknowledge your part in the drama as it unfolds.

Your choice is to act on your fears or to run from them. Can you see that the salvation of the world rests within your intentions to confront your personal fears? The lesson a Hitler teaches is that every time you are willing to confront that which was previously believed to be fearful, you have freed the world from one more harsh lesson. Your decision to face your fears makes more of a difference at this time than you can ever know.

If you wish to be depressed and fearful no more, go today and look into the corners and recesses of your being, into all the places you have secretly swept your fears with the hope of starving them. Fears are nourished in darkness. In the light of awareness they shrivel and die. Identify your fears and move toward them, let them guide you.

When your heart is heavy and your soul depressed, list those things you fear. You will know what to write. Simply say the word and they shall come forth. Call them out of the darkness and into the light. You will immediately feel a sense of peace and freedom. In your choosing to see truth, you will automatically lose your fear.

When your heart is heavy and your soul depressed, be still and allow your fears to well up within you. Though the mind will tell you they are large, they shall be as a speck of dust when you shine the light of true intention upon them.

## *Focus on Fear*

Know that all negative feelings regardless of how the mind identifies them are fear in disguise. Your greatest tool for recovery is awareness. See clearly that the vagueness of anxiety is really a fear of something, that jealousy is fear of loss, that depression is fear of expressing. Begin to see that the real culprit often masquerades in a socially acceptable form.

Understand that once you have unmasked the true cause of your discomfort by taking one small step toward overcoming your fear, one symbolic gesture within the power of your choice will put your fear on notice that you are ready to confront it in your life.

# *Pain*

*"The purpose of the illusion of pain is to
instruct through forgiveness, a healing
truth with unequaled power."*

The illusion of pain shall mark and guide your path; do not
miss the gifts it has for you. What you call pain represents the
absence of love for the particular situation which you are engaged
in, along with the emotion of fear. This experience called pain
– the absence of love combined with the feeling of fear – serves
as your guide to those areas of your life that require care and attention.

Like fear, pain is, in most situations, helpful. In some situations
pain is often initiated by self so as to balance out those things in
life not in keeping with your integritous nature. In the past you
have felt this type of pain as punishment, but it is only your deep
self attempting to stabilize and balance your life.

Pain in its most limited sense is a device of the ego to keep you
within prescribed safe boundaries. In the world you have created,
it appears to be normal to be in discomfort. Let us examine the
game the ego has set up so that you might experience the pain of
failure.

Pain in its purest form serves as a warning, a signal of things to
come, an experience that can protect and instruct you. If pain is
disregarded or you give no indication that you have understood

its message, the discomfort will worsen. It is your fear of the message contained within the pain that causes it to increase.

If, at the first indication of pain within your life, you acknowledge it, asking of it what it needs to teach and then loving that situation from which the pain has arisen, you will find that it diminishes in both its intensity and frequency. It is as if someone who has been entrusted with your protection has sounded an alarm – the warning device will continue until you heed its message.

This is true for emotional pain as well as physical pain. The purpose of the illusion of pain is to instruct through forgiveness, a healing truth with unequaled power.

Pain, as with all things learned on this plane, may be used for constructive purposes or for confirming limitation and lack. Pain, when used in its most vile form, has been stripped of all truth behind it. This pain may be the pain known as retaliation – the pain of attack, of guilt. It is pain inflicted upon another or self. Like all pain, this type represents the absence of love plus fear, but it also holds within its essence JUDGMENT. It is this pain inflicted on another that reflects the ego's attempts to avoid self-correction by passing judgment.

The pain you inflict on others and self in the name of righteousness brings you grave consequences. For lifetimes to come, you will attempt to balance your actions by receiving the same quality of pain you have given. This is law and it is just.

When you are in the midst of pain ask of it these questions. You will then recognize it by the answers it gives. Ask of your pain if it is warning or judgment, instruction or punishment, aiding or limiting growth, expanding or contracting your sense of self?

To overcome all pain you need only to confront it fearlessly and to remain open to the gift it offers you. Then give thanks for the miracle of consciousness that has allowed this communication to take place. EMBRACE YOUR PAIN.

If your pain represents judgment, punishment, or contracts your spirit ask from where this pain has come. It will always give you an accurate account. This type of pain will feel shallow in its intensity. Again you may eliminate this pain through the miracle of forgiveness – forgiveness of self.

Nothing is gained or learned through the prolonging of pain. Life is not meant to be painful. Other than fear, pain is the greatest illusion on earth. Without the creation of pain as punishment, of eternal damnation, as a way to correct other, it would simply be you living with no boundaries, with no fear, with no limits. That is a divine life and possible for each to experience.

Be afraid of pain no more, for to look at it in the light of love is to recognize the message it holds for you. Your pain is saying in its own way that the world is effortless, a place of beauty and joy manifested through action, a love made visible through creative energy. No longer choose to run from the lessons pain offers. Instead, look for the gift hidden within its message and know that you have taken a step toward establishing the kingdom of heaven on earth as you release yourself from pain.

# Focus on Pain

It is important for you to become aware of the type of pain you have. Focus directly on the pain whether emotional or physical. Sit still and dialogue with it.

Pain comes in two forms – either as a means of warning of imbalance or as punishment, such as guilt prescribed by your mind for sins believed to have been committed. The way to find out if the pain you experience is beneficial and a warning or punishment and judgment is to ask of it these questions.

1. Are you real or imaginary?

2. Are you warning or are you judgment?

3. Are you here for my instruction or correction?

4. Are you here to aid my growth or to limit it?

5. Do I really need to experience this pain or may I just let it go?

6. What is the message you have come to deliver to me?

# Anger and Guilt

*"Allow your pain to pass through you
calmly; no longer attempt to resist it
through the defense of anger."*

The ego resists seeing itself as vulnerable and denies the pain this avoidance produces through the use of anger. The mind portrays this anger as righteous, convincing you that you have been in some way injured or wronged, reinforcing your belief in your own limitation and promoting the cycle of dependency.

The mind uses anger as a diversionary tactic so you might not see the truth. When you are enraged you are no longer aware of options or choices.

Think upon the ways you exhibit your anger. What forms does it take? Against other through physical or mental abuse, or against self through the use of drugs or drink that take from you your own life force? You may even become angry at God or others wishing only to guide you. Regardless of the means chosen, anger shall always destroy your own peace.

Peace is your salvation and you are consuming it through anger. Anger is seen in the aura as the color red. As a primary color, it has the ability to alter radically the light contained in all other colors. The pure white light within you becomes tainted by your anger. You are literally lost in your own rage.

When you project your pain outward through anger you auto-

45

matically contract and become a partner with guilt. The mind will never allow you to exhibit anger without inflicting you with guilt. Guilt is the form of punishment exacted by the mind for your yielding to anger. Guilt is the control device originated by the mind to keep you within prescribed boundaries called limitations.

You allow this conquest for you believe that guilt is an absolution, a pardon from the supposed sin of anger. You reason that a display of guilt and remorse shall vindicate and show you to be properly repentant. This actually serves to perpetuate your behaviour. It is your belief that guilt has value as a means of correction, and so it actually permits you to continue acting in a hostile way.

The mind insists that so long as you suffer through guilt, you need correct none of your destructive behaviors. Guilt shall be considered payment in full for a crime you could never commit. Guilt is offered as a form of appeasement, but it is always your peace that is sacrificed. You can be abused and battered by the tyranny of your mind. The mind tells you that God's wrath and fury is great with a willingness to punish you. It is little wonder that you are fearful. The face of God we have seen looks nothing like the description given by your ego.

It is guilt that leads to depression of the soul. It is the depression in the soul that causes a collapse of the immune system. It is the collapse of the immune system that causes a disease within your being that leaches the life force from your essence.

Yet there is a gift that might be used for your freedom from the cycle of dependency – it is called forgiveness. Forgiveness was brought to this plane by Jesus. Forgiveness is the first principle in the stage of Transition found within the Cycle of Ascendancy. Jesus brought with him the possibility of Transition that leads away from Tradition and forgiveness is the path. To apologize further promotes the illusion of grievances and guilt. To forgive grants innocence and harmlessness, and so absolves you completely.

Fear brings you the illusion of pain that becomes anger when denied and excused through guilt. The result is a depression of the body and soul. These experiences are part of the cycle of dependency. Each of these stages of illusion are dependent upon your refusal to acknowledge and confront your fears. You consume your own life energy protecting your fears within this cycle.

You may disengage yourself from the destruction found in the cycle of dependency at any stage – simply choose again. Choose love over fear, joy over pain, peace over anger.

The pain you feel when you ignore your fears comes from the hurt the heart feels as you begin your descent into darkness and away from the light. If you experience pain, see that it is only a mask for your fear. Ask that you may see its true identity and when it shows you its face, do not run. Stand still and gaze upon it with love. Love will change its complexion.

Allow your pain to pass through you calmly; no longer attempt to resist it through the defense of anger. Break the cycle of dependency, beloved, so that you might be free to move into the Cycle of Ascendancy.

If you have gone beyond pain and are already into the stage of anger, then break the cycle where you find yourself. Request that the earth safely dispose of your hostility and violence. Channel the anger in a non-destructive way – away from other and self. No longer follow your anger mindlessly into the arms of guilt. Guilt is a futile and meaningless consumption of your energy that promotes even greater fear by masking your unique beauty and power.

Forgive yourself completely, and then consciously confront your underlying fears. You are dependent on nothing, for you are sufficient unto yourself, a divine emissary of God on a vital mission.

47

No longer deny your own ascended journey through the motion contained in this vicious cycle called dependency that leads nowhere. You shall now deliver yourself out of the darkness of fear through your ability to simply consciously choose again.

Behind peace, behind prosperity, behind tranquility, harmony, trust, joy, and faith stands only love. Behind greed, envy, jealousy, hatred, poverty, disease, and despair stands only fear. It is a masquerade devised by the ego to hide your choices. It is within your power to choose love over fear, light over darkness, connection over separation, peace over anger, forgiveness over guilt, life over death in all its forms.

# Focus on Awareness

Choose one thing currently in your life which produces within you a feeling of restriction or confinement, but in which you continue to remain due to your limiting beliefs or fears. Some of the areas you might consider are educational, social, or spiritual – your career, health, finances, relationships, parenting.

1.  Identify the area and then think about what form movement might take. Do not include any of your doubts, fears, considerations, reasons why you can't, justifications, rationales, or evaluations. Simply write down what you would like to have happen.

2.  Write the story of how you have come to where you are now in this particular area of your life. How did you feel about this situation in the beginning?

3.  Describe in detail how staying in this pattern makes you feel now.

Begin to see that the situation is not wrong nor are your feelings about it wrong. There is, in fact, nothing wrong with this picture; it is simply one that no longer meets your needs and it is time to move on. Begin to see the stages in your life clearly so that you might recognize the signals given to initiate movement. In this way you can begin to react to change as a natural part of life for in truth life is change and to live is to change.

# Depression

*"It is your destiny to be free forever from depression of the spirit and to live your life from a new perspective. A divine purpose has brought you to exactly this place in time."*

Depression is the only form of what could be considered original sin upon your plane of earth. It occurs in what we will term a natural way, for you are all born with it innately in your bodies, and because of the thoughts and actions of those who have lived before, it surrounds the earth as a shroud called collective consciousness.

When your divine spirit, with all the capabilities of a god, passes through into embodiment, certain portions of the soul lower their vibratory level. It is specifically that portion of the soul's essence that forms itself into physical mass that begins to slow down its rotation in order to exhibit physical characteristics.

It is in this way that the soul is directly responsible for the physical qualities taken on by the body. It is in this process that the soul manifests choice in the life to come. With only a little assistance you would all remember that this is a painful process, for it is that part of the soul that has agreed to embody that must literally DEPRESS itself into the contraction called form.

So then DEPRESSION is most assuredly something to be reckoned with upon your emergence into this new world as well as within your own physical body. This type of natural depression is familiar to all who have chosen this life form and can be overcome with little difficulty by simple physical movement. Since this type of depression originated through the compressing of the spirit, you may alleviate the problem through a reversal. Allow the body to move. It is in this way that the portion of the soul expressing as physical mass might experience expansion once again.

Along with depression as an innate quality of the experience known as embodiment, there are also all of the other human emotions including the lower ones – hatred, envy, greed, anger, fear, as well as the higher ones – compassion, joy, gratitude, peace, and love.

The lower order of emotions are literally more dense in their molecular structure and as such attach themselves most easily to that portion of the soul that has chosen to contract itself for the purpose of embodiment. It is the higher order of emotions that are closer to the vibration of light and so instead attach themselves to the lessons learned by the soul during each subsequent lifetime.

It is for this reason that those souls incarnating for the first time upon this plane express most easily the lower emotions. Their experiences and lessons have been limited and so they do not attract to them the higher vibration of emotions.

You have all experienced the soul's passing through this condition of depressing in order to gain physical form or you could not be here. Because you have contracted a portion of your own spirit you each are exposed to the quality of depression within your lives.

In addition to the natural depression literally born into the process of life on earth, there are also individual circumstances that the soul has chosen to experience in order to understand its own nature and its purpose.

You have all experienced these types of depression as well as the

51

lower order of emotions. It has been through your willingness to continue with your lessons upon this plane that you have now attracted the higher ones and now feel more balanced. Through your many and varied lifetimes you have each ingeniously learned ways of transmuting depression into positive action.

The final depression, the depression that most of you who read these words experience, is the depression experienced as an old soul. This feeling is one of frustration. It is the frustration an old soul experiences when it has come very close to understanding the truth and yet has not the courage to sustain its quest – so then it must again incarnate another lifetime.

Depression within the old soul may correctly be viewed as a great tool to experience final freedom. For eventually the soul will dictate to the limited personality its overriding discontent with the situation and will seek to dwell within a superior one.

It is amazing how long you will remain within the confusion of depression rather than venture forward into the clarity of commitment. Your endurance of and tolerance for pain is beyond our comprehension. So reluctant are you to release the grip that causes your soul to become contracted and weak that you would even prefer disease and death.

To release your depression as old souls you must recognize your spirit's desire to find and experience ITS OWN TRUTH. This individualized expression of truth can never be found within the confines of what the ego dictates as acceptable behaviour – and because of this you will forever feel at odds here on the earth plane.

What appears to be safe and acceptable behaviour to the limited mind, is in fact the quickest route to immobility and stagnation for your soul. The eventual outcome is always the same – death. Often when the soul is consistently disregarded, it becomes literally one-dimensional within the life force it has chosen to experi-

52

ence and, beloved, one dimension does not equate successfully in a three-dimensional world. So it becomes necessary to exit.

When the ego is allowed to press its version of reality upon the soul, the spirit is literally depressed and the desire and drive to expand is flattened. It quite truthfully has no depth, only mass.

The old soul is more prone to this type of ailment. It often takes lifetimes to learn that there is nothing to fear and that the two things the ego would have you believe are enemies (CHANGE and MOVEMENT) are actually mechanisms for assistance, feeding you with life and hope.

Movement here means not the frenzied confusion that can consume your day – the endless lists of things to accomplish. Rather, it is a song sung by the spirit, a song of spontaneity and freedom. Each of you will hear this song differently, for it will not sound the same from season to season. As the tune changes so will the direction of movement that comes from it.

Once the soul has experienced and conquered, once it has understood as well as taught, then will it wish for a change.

If change does not occur, then stagnation will set in. If your spirit is to remain in a multidimensional state, it must move and change. – this multidimensional soul will then serve as an example and be allowed to out picture to the world its beauty and wisdom.

There are those who see aspects of life as simply black and white, who disregard their hearts in favor of their heads. These individuals are losing the dimensional properties needed in order to experience their inner TRUTH. You can never see through the illusions of this plane if you succumb to your fear of movement and change. You may not see your TRUTH if the soul is drained of its dimensional properties through depression.

Please see clearly that the soul always asks for change, for challenge, for new understandings. Once it has conquered these, it seeks them again in another form. This seeking of your soul will lead you beyond the hundreds of lifetimes it has lived in order that you might fully experience aspects of life as you progress on the way to the ultimate understanding – there is no more to experience here.

When the soul has satisfied itself completely, it will give you the last experience needed in order to produce total understanding. It is this final experience where each of you now finds yourself and it is the process of Balance.

Your soul has tried on every illusion ever wished for and never tired of its part, it has walked this earth taking on roles and becoming immersed in dramas that were but dreams and never once wished to wake. Now, however, the same desire that delivered you to this door of time/space through which you walked consciously and deliberately at the beginning of time as you count it, will now choose to leave and become unified with the light.

It is law that you leave this plane the same way you came. The same desires that caused you to incarnate here have brought you full circle and you now long to experience the freedom from which you came. You wish to go home to the Source and the soul shall show you how, and for many it will occur this lifetime.

There is but one more illusion the soul chooses to cast itself in. We shall call it a cameo role for it is small in duration, but one that is large in impact and truly worthy of the part you are to play. You all shall know your lines in this particular drama for the still small voice is your prompter.

It is your destiny to facilitate, through the raising of your vibration, the coming New Age. It is your destiny to allow your spirit to expand and thus to lead with your personality in tow. It is your destiny to be free forever from depression of the spirit and to live your life from a new perspective. A divine purpose has brought you to exactly this place in time.

Move through each day of your life with the assurance that your vision is clear. The exchange you are about to make is a perfect one – your clarity for another's illusion. It is now your destiny to see through fear, doubt, anger, pain, greed, jealousy, and guilt. Beloved beloved, know that your willingness to express the needs of the soul will forever free you from depression.

No longer fear to express your pain. Know that to express is to release yourself forever from the grip of a foe whose only wish is to to keep you from experiencing your own unlimitedness.

In the days to come your new willingness to express self will be seen easily among the thoughts that come to you seemingly from nowhere. But be not deceived, they come from the Source of all things and their expression is appropriate upon this path.

Depression is a delusion manifested as a heaviness upon the heart that longs for expansion. When the heart is heavy, your soul begins to lower its vibratory level and you experience greater depression.

It is your purpose to prepare your vessel, your body, for the higher rate of frequency that is the foretelling of the Maitraya. For this reason you shall be able to forever exorcise yourself of the residue of lifetimes of depression.

Expression shall be the path upon which you will find your release from depression. When you hear us speak, act and move in a way that indicates understanding on your part – this will be called faith. In this way shall we be partners in the joint intention of overthrowing a dictator – called depression – that has for too long held your mind and body captive.

There are those who feel this message of depression speaks not to them. Be not deceived for you could not be upon this plane of earth without suffering from this condition. You who feel no discomfort at this message, you are in the most serious danger, for your ego believes itself to be superior and will seek to disregard our promptings.

Your bodies are tools for you to use to open the way for new energy now available. You must make space within yourselves by consciously expressing depression in order to welcome this new energy onto the earth plane.

Those who make no effort to listen will make no room and will not be light bearers. It is your choice – it has always been your choice. Listen with new ears and know that you are not alone and that you are greatly loved for the courage with which you now undertake to complete your destiny.

# Focus on Depression

Depression is a result of not paying sufficient attention to the spirit within, neglect which causes a feeling of dejection. It takes courage and commitment to overcome depression.

It is essential that you locate the fears in your life and begin to move towards expression. It may be as simple as risking disapproval by telling someone the truth. To overcome the darkness of depression you must only make a move toward the light. If you do not know how, just ask yourself the question "What am I afraid of?" and listen to the answer that comes from intuition, for that will be your next step. In that message is the miracle that you have been asking for in your life.

# Disease

*"The choice to experience health is made
by you daily through your beliefs, your
attitudes, your thoughts and decisions."*

What you consider disease is not foreign to the body. All diseases that ever were and will yet be, exist right now within you, although the state in which they reside is nonintrusive. You decide when and what "disease" you will choose to experience by depressing the immune system, which is responsible for maintaining health and well-being within your body through balance. The organisms called disease hosted within your body are kept in check until there occurs a "depression" within the system. Your emotional and mental disposition regulate the immune system and your attitude toward the life being lived is responsible for the longevity and health that is to be yours.

Your body becomes the battleground for the war waged between the illusion of fear and the truth found in love. Your choice is contraction or expansion. When you are in contraction you depress your system and literally contract with disease.

Do not fear disease, for fear attracts negativity. Disease feeds upon fear and causes it to spread. If it is your wish not to experience disease, do not dwell with fear. Instead live your life from a position of courage and conviction. The cure for all disease upon your planet is a preventive rather than curative formula. Go toward your fears and overcome them. In this way you will send a message to your body that there is only love left.

With your willingness to confront your fears you will literally create a new truth within you that will stimulate a chemical substance to be released that will promote life.

Begin to live your life fearlessly without resentment, without hostility, without guilt, without jealousy or envy. This will align you with truth and so bring you into the state called health.

To lose these lower emotions and instead gain a life of peace and balance is to be by definition without disease in your life. It is again quite simply a choice – your choice. The choice to experience health is made by you daily through your beliefs, your attitudes, your thoughts and decisions.

The being that is you is so impeccable, so strictly honest and integritous that it always gives you the result for which you are looking. If you feel ill at ease within your life, you will quite literally out picture this experience in your body through disease.

So it is in this way that you will become your own practitioner. For those who wish not to experience the message found in disease your cure is found in your love of self. Love yourself, love your life, love your choices – all of them, regardless of how the world and others may judge you. Health is always found in the message given you by the still small voice within. Follow your intuition and allow it to direct you toward radiant health. Choose health and be a peaceful warrior against the beliefs the world holds of pain and suffering, of disease and death.

# Focus on Disease

If you are currently suffering from a physical ailment attempt to see it as an aspect of yourself instead of something separate and foreign. Acceptance may be the interim step between having the disease and healing it.

If the illness you are experiencing is not life threatening or disabling, this exercise is, of course, easier to do. Start with something small like a headache, a cold, indigestion, or a blemish. Perhaps you can see this symptom as a signal from inside of yourself sent as a messenger to alert you. Maybe that message is just to rest, or to relax, or to release.

In no way is this exercise meant to minimize your situation. Nor is this exercise meant to get you to experience blame for "causing or creating" it. And, obviously this exercise is not meant to take the place of medical attention. Far from it. What I am asking is that you begin to stop just for a moment and do something different in order to learn something new. Do not despise, drug, deny, or distance yourself from your ailment.

You are your own internal physician. Now is the time to start the intuitive process that may make you more adept at assisting in your own healing.

1. Make a space in yourself to accept this ailment-- for this moment.

2. Try to talk with it and listen to the response regardless of how silly it sounds.

3. Act with serious intent on anything you learn from that dialogue.

4. Would you be willing to make an exchange for your ailment? Make a list of the things you might be willing to add to your

life (such as peace, serenity, exercise), or release from your life(such as stress, job, anxiety...) in order to make that exchange for healing?

# Aging

*"Aging is directly related to the emotion
of fear, the most damaging illusion found
upon this plane. When fear is invited
into your being, debilitating toxins are
released as this emotion interacts with the
chemical structure of your physical body."*

Aging, a most misunderstood aspect within the cycle of life, was never to happen. It is yet another example of how the physical body rids itself of your negative emotions, your depression, repression, and regrets.

Aging is not mandatory. There are many upon your plane who age little, yet they are in the minority and so do not come forth willingly for they would be seen as oddities. The process you consider a lifetime was to be undertaken during the span of several hundred years.

Do not be fooled into thinking that this condensation of time has occurred because you have lived a good full life, utilizing each precious second. The truth is exactly the opposite.

The less life force you extract from each experience while within physical form, the more the body is then asked to compensate for your disuse. It is the body that is sacrificed so as to compensate for the soul's dissatisfaction with the life being lived.

There is within you a very sophisticated mechanism that shall translate onto the body the soul's evaluation of the life being lived. This occurs through the release of chemical electrostimulants within the brain. If these stimulants send a message that life is fulfilling, something loved and enjoyed, the body responds to the energy and these feelings automatically prepare your being to accept more life.

However, the opposite is also possible. If the ego is given the opportunity to override the spirit of the soul with fearful imaginings, doubts, and hostility, a chemical decomposition begins, shutting out life itself.

We have stated in the past that if the spirit be consciously disregarded then it is up to the body to find a way to process this literal contraction.

Depending on how strongly the message is relayed, the body determines the number and intensity of steps necessary to carry out the execution – all this, with the hope of sending you a visible message so that you might choose a different future and so reverse your present course.

When you resist your spirit's inner drive for individual expression and experience, there occurs a physical transmission within the synapses of your brain that is deciphered as limitation and transcribed as such upon the body. Know that even the subtle messages received daily will eventually cause a total disintegration of your apparatus.

Aging might be slow and subtle or a quick debilitating attack upon your life force.

Wrinkles are the body's way of allowing you to examine visually the activities your soul has missed, opportunities disregarded, actions not taken. Wrinkles indicate that life was not fully lived so there is a literal break in the otherwise smooth complexion, just as there has been a break in the continuity of the life force.

63

The body is a miracle of design and creation that is too often taken for granted until it is too late. The body never lies to you; you are able to read the nature of the individual's love of self from the integrity of the body.

It is not our wish that you use this information as yet another way to judge others. Instead look only in the mirror at your own reflection. This self-observation may be achieved in two ways. The first is through the use of your mirrors and a sensitive rather than critical look at what your reflection may show you. Know that those things the body reflects outwardly are an indication of an inner message and should be interpreted literally.

The second way you may observe self is to use your relationship with other as your mirror. This type of observation comes most easily to you, for you have all played this game called projection and judgment. Yet have you stopped just short of attaining any valuable personal information. We ask now that when you judge another for any reason, you take careful note of your own sensitivities to what is courageously being shown to you. There is valuable awareness when you ask of self: what part of the reflection I am being shown am I unable to love in myself?

Aging is directly related to the emotion of fear, the most damaging illusion found upon this plane. When fear is invited into your being, debilitating toxins are released as this emotion interacts with the chemical structure of your physical body. If fear, the grandest illusion on this plane, is believed as a truth and then taken into the body, it releases the chemical equivalent decoded as limitation and hopelessness. That which is hopeless quickly becomes abandoned.

Fear may be experienced through minor incidents or major life issues. Regardless, it always registers within the body as dysfunction and is translated as disease. There is no other way for the body to process the enormity of the lie called fear.

If there is a secret of life, it is to go toward those things received by the mind as fearful, do those things that are feared. Your fears are your guides, showing you the twists and turns of your inner path.

Follow your fears and you will breath more easily. Challenge your fearful imaginings and feel the clarity of vision being restored to your eyes, a clarity that allows you to see through the illusions that surround you.

When you witness the release from fear and its actual grip of death over the body, you will never again submit it to such abuse. You will be able to choose experiences that strengthen the body through joy, health, happiness, and love.

Watch as your body decodes the information contained within the emotions of gratitude and celebration. Feel the totally expanding energy as it moves through your entire being sending with it the message of valued life and your desire to participate fully in all of it. Ultimately, your body will receive the message that you wish to continue the experience of life. You determine how long this life shall be.

Choose life or death by moving toward peace or into resistance. Know that it is your choice. Be aware that the emotions you invite into your body determine its longevity.

Love yourself fully. Experience all your spirit wishes and receive the joy this will bring. Have no fears, for everything upon this plane is here for your learning and as such is valuable. There is nothing here to harm you; only your fear and hostility toward your own creative life force can do that.

Go and be joyous and by so doing you will live each moment as if it were a lifetime. Your life then will be full of meaning and promise and as such will be timeless. The eternal life force of the universe moves through you each moment; receive its unique message and fulfill your destiny by simply living as an open tributary of that source.

# Focus on Aging

Those who are the most concerned with growing old and aging were the first to relinquish their childhood for what appeared to be the benefits of being adults. In the process of "growing up" you have abandoned the child within that keeps you young. Youth and maturity are not exclusive.

If you would like to inherit the Kingdom of Heaven you must become as little children – childlike not childish. Look at what you and your friends do when you get together – eat, drink, and talk. Look at what your children do – fantasize, laugh, run, play, jump.

Being active keeps you engaged in life and feeling young.

Go today and be more childlike with yourself. Heal the child that was "prematurely" abandoned within you.

Hug yourself as if you were your own mother. Give yourself permission to do one thing today that is without serious purpose. If you have a child close by give them an hour and allow them to design what you do together. Watch as your mind will resist and complain, but once involved notice how your heart responds and the joy of being young at play.

# Death

*"Death is not an end to life; it is merely*
*a different vantage point from which*
*your consciousness might gain a new*
*perspective on life."*

Death is the greatest illusion, the greatest fear upon this plane and so when understood, it holds the greatest learning. In order to experience ongoing progressive life you must not exclude any part, especially not your exiting. It is only through the confrontation of this, the greatest illusion ever created by man, that you may begin to embrace that which will never pass away – your own divine spirit.

Upon your plane birth and death cannot be separated. To engage in one is to disengage through the other. In this absolute realization will you find your undeniable divinity known as Creation and through it experience everlasting life.

There is much confusion, fear, ignorance, and resistance to this particular part of the cycle of life called by you as death. Yet these emotions are the very things which keep you from participating with full abandon in the life you are now living. You tiptoe around your passions and desires so as not to disturb the sleeping dragon of death, hoping it might forget and let you live one more day. You roll over and play dead well before your time, beloved, in the hopes that you will be somehow overlooked when the grim reaper makes his final tally.

We have watched all of you for hundreds of lifetimes, ingressing onto this plane through birth and egressing from her through death. beloved, we will tell you that you are always dissatisfied with whatever particular moment you find yourself within. By this we mean that when you are in body you are fearful and anxious creatures, attempting all means of escape from the human condition. Rather than live life, you merely cope and survive. You know precisely the substances and harmful experiences in which you engage daily that lead directly to your own death. There is no mystery, so stop pretending; there are no accidents nor random occurrences. Everything is a choice, conscious or otherwise.

You forego many wondrous experiences in your attempts to sedate yourself. You seek any means of diversion so as to become unconscious to the glorious moment. The final and greatest diversion of consciousness is found in the fantasy of your own death. You have devised death as the ultimate means of escape. On one hand you fear it unreasonably; on the other you prematurely invite it into your life through your choices.

So then, beloved, you finally succeed, through years of abuse and neglect, through hostility and suffering, to pass from the limitation of physical form into the freedom of spirit. But instead of being happy, you find yourself frustrated. You long to live again – knowing what you now know. You long to live through the senses again. You long once again for the boundaries provided by the body and the predictability provided by earth. When you are in form you lament your limitations and when you are spirit you mourn for matter and mass.

Endlessly have we watched this cycle of confusion. Never are you fully present either in body or in ethers. Instead, you are reluctant, resistant, complaining, and ineffective upon whichever plane you find yourself. In a word, beloved, you are uncommitted. A commitment to the totality of the experience comes from the acceptance of the perfection in the moment – wherever that moment is found.

Remember that all causes have effects, whatever you shall sow so shall you also reap, and contained within each seed lies the entirety of the final outcome. A commitment to the whole process known as your life experience, regardless of the stage in which you find yourself, holds within it the lesson of mastery.

The experience of your death will be similar to the experience of your life. If you find your life to be unsatisfactory so will be your death. Although it appears that all on this plane die, not all deaths are the same. Just as the qualities of all lives are not the same, so is it true of death. Because you believe life to be over at death, you have given little thought or concern to the impact that life has upon your passing. Heaven and hell is your own devising and they may exist upon any and all planes that you find yourself – there is no escape.

We can assure you, your existence as consciousness does not end through the experience of death. No longer take the view that death is a refuge in which you may attain automatic peace and absolute tranquility as your final resting place. Instead, know that what you sow upon this, the physical plane, will manifest once again upon the next. There is no place you may run from your own thoughts, words, or deeds.

This is not a punishment, beloved, it is a promise. If your account-ability seems to be a punishment rather than a promise of possi-bility, then you have reason to worry.

Death is not an end to life; it is merely a different vantage point from which your consciousness might gain a new perspective. Nor is birth the beginning to life; it is merely a different vantage point from which your consciousness might gain a new perspec-tive. Birth and death are simply synonymous terms. They repre-sent a part of the process in which you find yourself engaged for the purpose of understanding – Expansive Life. It is essential to your own evolution towards inner wholeness that you now identify all stages of your life as being part of one continuous and eternal cycle. Division and separation shall no longer be permissible.

Yet there are those who no longer physically participate in, nor are they even drawn to this dream upon earth. Those entities of which we count ourselves a part, no longer engage in the ceremony of birth and death, yet do we continue to experience life. For life is consciousness expressing as expansive awareness. Consciousness does not die at death. Nor is it born at birth. *Consciousness is not limited except by your perception of it.*

Life is eternal, ongoing, dynamic, and creative in its response to itself. Life is the gift given freely to you from God's grace. You cannot earn your living as you believe. Living and labour are quite different. Since the mind believes in struggle it has sold you on the similarities. You are granted the gift of life and you are a precious piece, a facet within the gem of humanity.

You cannot die, you have not failed, and loss is impossible. Death is a collectively agreed upon experience unique to earth. In the past it has been your wish to share this experience with those of your fellows, for you have been gregarious. Soon in your time and by your counting all that has come before will not necessarily come again. Those who wish to experience differently may simply choose to do so.

Yet be clear, you may not make this choice away from death out of fear of it. Rather must you fearlessly choose life in all the forms that experience may hold for you. For what your consciousness has not yet fully understood and resolved to its satisfaction, will it always choose to attract to it. By this we mean that you may only choose eternal life if and when you have embraced death and dying. If you love the living as much as the dying then you will be balanced in your being.

This is called paradox, a catch 22, is it not? For when you have fearlessly resolved that all aspects of life are absolutely acceptable, then you would certainly be willing to release yourself into, rather than resist the cycle called death – and because that is the case you will no longer find it necessary to do so. There will however be a difference in the feeling tone and the quality of that life being lived – from one of fear to one of love. To be reborn you must be willing to die. That loving acceptance, that willingness to embrace all aspects of one's life equally, holds within it the chemical stimulants that make longevity a joy.

There is no "catch" in God's contract with you, There is no wish to snag you. Instead, this confusion is only the other side of illusion. The other side of illusion is reality and they exist simultaneously upon this plane. What is real may never be threatened and what is illusion does not exist except on this planet. You have been granted free will, and with it your destiny; in which belief system do you wish to participate?

You wish to live forever only because you are so afraid of dying. The ego believes that if you do not live fully you will somehow elude death or perhaps not miss life so much. So the ego teaches fear and lack. Yet it is the life lived in quiet desperation that causes spirit to long to escape. It is your very fear of the unknown called death that continues to call you to it for reasons of clarification. The lives you lead are constricted by fear and struggle and as such are not even worth the living, so you leave. Death is simply spirit seeking a premature escape from the boredom of the life chosen.

If you were not afraid of dying you would live your lives fearlessly and would therefore create a glorious edifice to everlasting life in each and every perfect moment. That life would then be worthy of being enjoyed for eternity and eternity would be experienced in each moment. Passing from this plane then would be a conscious choice of no more consequence than whether you should move to the country or stay in the city.

We will tell you that because you have not gained the access of your own past life recall, you are continuously forgetting how to die and so your passings are awkward and messy, causing a great deal of trauma, confusion, and chaos to all those concerned.

Since many of you do not even believe that consciousness continues after death, those who are there to assist you find it most difficult to convince you that you have truly passed over. You are much like a drowning person who has forgotten they can swim and in their panic is out of control flailing around in fear and confusion.

Death as an experience is to be both dignified and valuable as a learning to your essence. Begin to allow for all the positive possibilities of the process of passing. In this way you will enlarge your own capacity for unlimitedness and fearlessness and so will create within self the desire to participate more completely in the ongoing spectacle of progressive life.

One part of life on this planet is called practicing. It is here on earth that you get to experience things over and over. Before you die, beloved, you will be asked to bury others. From this experience you can glean great wisdom and insight as well as assist a fellow traveler. Do not demand they remain, do not deceive them, do not deny their experience. Instead, ask them what they need of you, be with them completely, affirm their ability to transit.

The mind will insist there are contradictions in what we say and we will tell you it seems to the mind to be the truth. In the past these issues were spoken in parables, for not all were ready to hear. Now we use other to transcribe the word through print so when read you hear only your voice. It is talking to you.

Meditate upon the words we communicate as well as those spoken long ago. In your heart you will hear no conflict. *'Lord, grant that I may not so much seek to be consoled as to console, to be understood as to understand, to be loved as to love, for it is in the giving that we receive, it is in pardoning that we are forgiven, and it is in dying that we are born to Eternal life.'*

73

It is now time to allow to pass from your being all the lies that have limited and kept you bound hopelessly to the cycle of death and destruction. Slay your fear, your envy, your greed, guilt, anger, jealousy, and hate, so that you will finally be free to live forever in peace, prosperity, harmony, joy, and love. This is a simple choice found in the moment-to-moment decisions and reactions. Choose love over fear, faith over doubt, light over darkness, joy over sorrow, and you will then have victory over death and a life that is worth living forever.

## Focus on Death

Death is only a final resting place for those who have been dying slowly for decades. It is not death but life you are afraid of. Go these days and live each day as if it were your last, but love as if you were to live forever, for in reality, this is exactly as it is.

What have you been waiting to do, to be, to see, and to say? DO IT NOW!!! In the doing you will begin to feel the power of purpose. You have come to this planet for a purpose – to live. When you fulfill that purpose, you receive renewed life; when you refuse your purpose, you relinquish life.

Death is a wondrous perspective from which to view the value of this life. Use it not in dread, but to distinguish what you want to spend your precious time pursuing upon this planet.

No one on earth has the power to prevent you from living life – only you can do that. This week become aware of all the ways you limit your life, while you simultaneously deceive yourself about death. It is not death nor the passing of loved ones that makes you mourn; it is the sorrow the self feels for a life gone unlived.

# TRANSITION

# Receptivity to Change

*"That which you do not love you cannot
leave; yet if you are afraid to leave you
cannot stay."*

Greetings to those hearty souls now upon the Path of Ascendancy. Tradition holds within it the most easily accessible roads, for the routes found there are well worn and thoroughly traveled. Yet that is not your way, for you have chosen a course that is uncharted. Your heart shall serve as your compass directing you toward Transition and a most magical journey awaits you. You are in Transition when you have "let go" or "given up" and feel a deep need for new understanding. The free fall of Transition allows you to discover new dreams and desires that you were unable to see while still within the confines of Tradition. Your dreams and desires seek to make themselves visible to you through the still small voice that often goes unheard because of your focus on the noise and commotion of the world.

Yet both of these stages hold within them dangers for you. In Tradition there is a danger that you may well stay too long and so find it necessary to create some catastrophe in order to effect movement in your life. In Transition there is a danger that you will not stay long enough and instead be lured back into Tradition by a mind anxious to return to the illusion of safety.

For many this time in Transition is often the most frightening. There are those who because of their traditional background are unable to relax and wait, to float and be free.

79

Instead they listen to the "shoulds" and the "ought tos" of both their ego and those who have remained behind. If the pressure is sufficient they rush back into Tradition at the first sign of ambiguity.

Beware, for it is during the time spent in Transition that Tradition may be disguised as Transformation. Remember that during the stage of Transition the mind will appear to be at its most logical. The mind will seem to support wholeheartedly your decision to have left Tradition, congratulating you in fact for your courage, your fortitude and clarity. Yet be not deceived, for in reality the mind wishes only to have you return to the security of Tradition.

It is at this point that you are given a test that if taken will fix your feet firmly upon the path toward Transformation. Should you, however, be swayed by your mind and prematurely move back into Tradition, you will then send a message to your spirit that will be equated with the feeling of hopelessness. Remember before you fail this test that when a message of hopelessness is translated by the spirit into the body it is always decoded as depression, disease, and eventually death. So the price paid by the body for the security of the ego is very great indeed.

It can ease your transition if you will become aware that in this stage there is much anxiety for the mind. It is essential if you are to complete this stage in the Cycle of Ascendancy that you begin to resolve your own impatience before you can move beyond it.

Before you can begin to move toward Transformation you must come to love the stage of Transition so that you may depart upon your journey. Your spirit asks to receive the available light found in each new experience, and Transition is no exception. That which you do not love you cannot leave; yet if you are afraid to leave you cannot stay.

To explain better the characteristics found in both Tradition and Transition we wish to make use of the metaphor of space. There is a need for man to venture out, to reach beyond his own limited experience, into realms of the unexplored. In this way does he attempt to learn more about his own capabilities. Space provides you with an opportunity to project yourselves out of your earthbound experience, to reach toward the heavens in an effort to expand beyond your own limitations.

In order to do this, however, it has been necessary to create a vehicle that might withstand the force and the heat that is generated from inside your atmosphere. What the vehicle experiences as gravity, beloved, might be seen by you as nothing more than the collective consciousness called Tradition attempting to hold you back.

If you are to overcome this gravitational pull of Tradition, it is essential that your vehicle be able to sustain substantial external pressure. It is within this crucial stage of your mission that you encounter the greatest atmospheric resistance and consequently must expend the largest portion of your fuel or energy supply.

The final stages of Tradition are experienced by your being as a need to explore, to break free from the known, to overcome the self-imposed limitations that now hold you down, to actually propel yourself beyond what has already been fully experienced. During this period you shall feel a call to explore that initiates the drive or force necessary to break through your own resistance.

When the craft finally exerts enough force to break through the gravitational pull, it then finds that it needs very little effort in order to continue its forward movement. Quite literally, the vehicle receives a push, a boost from the universe. There is no resistance found in this stage, which is motionless, soundless, and weightless. Time and space are altered here. Time flows and space floats. The force necessary to propel you through the first stage now creates within the second one a momentum that affords you effortlessness.

This then is Transition and you shall recognize your entry therein by its unique characteristics: peace, tranquility, silence, receptivity, patience, calmness, and acceptance. You float free within her, open to all that is about to come. There is no need for frantic or strenuous movement, for the momentum you have generated from your exiting out of Tradition will carry you safely all the way into Transformation.

In Transition time will be altered and by comparison the trip may appear to be interminably slow.

Remember, however, that once you have left Tradition, the speed of your journey is totally irrelevant to its successful outcome. While within Transition your only concern, beloved, is to silence the ungrounded fears of the mind. Turn your energy and attention toward a new direction and instead listen to a different voice, one that speaks to you of initiations and new beginnings rather than of compromises and justifications.

Before your departure from Tradition realize fully that there will be a time spent within Transition that will be expressed by the soul as great relief for taking the first step toward the light. Do nothing while in Transition and know that your willingness to be still shall point toward a new direction. To listen, to relax, to be still, to be open – it is in this way that you are preparing for your entry into Transformation.

The outer world believes that "something is always better than nothing," but quite often this is not so. Reverse your priorities while in Transition – question what the outer world tells you is of value.

Transition is a glorious road that shall open new avenues for you. It is during Transition that expansion is experienced through no effort. Enjoy this respite on the way toward your discovery of Transformation. Soon all of your efforts will be focused on navigating the unfamiliar surface of Transformation. Enjoy the rest you receive during the lull of Transition.

In the past we have stated that the world supports the order that if you have things in your life you can then do what you want so you might be happy. During Transformation you will recognize that you must only be who you are, so that you might do less if you are to have all that you need. Yet while in Transition you only need to be still, do nothing, and have faith.

Use the tools of the metaphor, the symbol, and the ceremony to help guide you through the changes that wait for you. Each of these has an impact upon the psyche.

Together they translate into an ancient language the soul remembers and understands. When the feeling tone they create is allowed to enter your being, your life will shift, becoming more open to change.

Call upon the tree as symbol to serve you in Transition as you become more open to change. The trees, those magnificent giants that serve as silent providers to the earth plane, are wise and patient, balanced and centered. This is what you will receive when you humble yourself to ask for their gifts.

Reaching deep into the earth itself, the tree's long roots pull sustenance upward into her exposed extremities. Then reaching upward with outstretched arms she pulls energy downward from the heavens into limbs and leaves. Your trees are great mediators upon your plane, serving each day between spirit and substance – between mother earth and father sky.

The tree willingly accepts your exhalation and then easily transmutes what is unused by you back into the precious substance called oxygen. You are in relationship with the tree, dependent upon her for the basics of your existence: shelter, food, and air.

The tree is a silent server, a peaceful observer of your world. She asks little of you and yet appreciates anything you might give her in passing.

Although the tree moves through endless cycles of life and death, she is a master without motion. Standing erect she possesses profound wisdom and true humility. She accepts the inevitable as well as the perfection found in all patterns of her life. She is unchanged by the passing of hundreds of seasons.

Look to the tree then as a symbol of Transition. For she is very much of the earth as she reaches toward the stars. Grounded, yet always growing and expanding, she embodies peace, grace, and serenity. Though the winds of change may attempt to sway her with their endless motion, she remains steadfast to her own commitment to remain still. She is your teacher, beloved. Listen to her wisdom so that your life might be centered, grounded, nourished, balanced, and harmonious.

Use an abandoned leaf as a symbol of those things that are no longer necessary in your life. Once vital and essential to your being, the life of the leaf has been used up and the tree lets it go. Write upon the dead leaf those things in your life ready to pass away. Place these leaves then upon a fire that will create a transition from substance to spirit. In that fire any negativity will be transmuted and then released into a more positive form.

On another leaf, we ask that you write those things you wish to hold on to in your life, things you wish to encourage to retain in your life. Then tie these prayer leaves to a tree, uniting them with their creator, just as your prayers unite you with the source of all creation.

Finally we will ask that you choose an acorn – the symbol of rebirth, of continuation, the promise of growth. Plant this seed into the earth along with your prayers. Know that what you ask with sincerity will be delivered to you with promptness. Know that the divine spirit inherent in all life now grants you absolute abundance so that all your dreams, desires, and wishes might mature, grow strong, and bear fruit as will this seed.

## *Focus on Transition*

To know in which direction you are headed, you must sense where you are and see where you have been. It is time to assess the patterns that have led to the paths taken in your life.

Begin to keep a journal of the times in your life when you felt movement that eventually resulted in success. Write down the successes you have had in your life. Focus on the things you have had to let go in order to achieve them. Perhaps you had to let go of a fear, or let go of one job to get a better one, or let go of a belief you held.

See that you have already traveled within the Cycle of Ascendancy even if unknowingly. Begin to recognize these patterns of change and growth in your life and what precipitates them so that in the future you will find the terrain you are crossing familiar. Transition is a time of observation and reflection, of receptivity as well as release. Be still, do nothing, have faith.

# Change

*"The soul sees change as the path to the
wholeness it seeks to rejoin."*

You may choose Tradition over the experiences of Transition
and Transformation for a long, painful time, but there will come
a time when the path toward movement and change is selected
to overcome stagnation and decay. Even then, growth and expansion, known as the cycle of life upon this planet, may be experienced by the ego as loss and pain.

Growth takes place in every area of your life. It may come as an
easy flow from the understanding of the rightness of the situation, or it may be felt as a wrenching away, a trauma experienced
because of your refusal to let go of what you view as traditional
action or thought.

In the first instance, the knowingness for change will come from
inside of self and be effected effortlessly outward into the waiting
world. In the second, change will appear to be a force from outside yourself acting upon you.

In either case the opening to change will begin as a small, still
voice within you, which will begin to stir, prompt, cajole, and
move. It is at this point that you have a choice: to move upon its
promptings, or to turn away and disregard it.

In situations where growth is deemed necessary by the soul but
goes unheeded by the ego, you will devise some means to cause

that movement to occur that will be in keeping with your essential core belief of how the world operates and your place within it.

If it is your belief that the world is hostile or that the people in it take advantage of you, then when a change is necessary in your life you will create a drama that will support and reinforce this core belief.

Much of what appears to you to be personal tragedy upon your plane of earth is in reality, nothing more than an unwillingness on the part of the personality to listen to the wishes of the deep self. In this way does it set up the drama for movement.

The ego shall have a view of the purpose of life that is forever in direct conflict with that of the soul's. The ego's major wish is for the safe, the known, and the secure.

The soul, in its absolute knowingness of its indestructibility, wishes only for growth, expansion, and new challenges so it may express its unlimitedness. The soul sees change as the path to the wholeness it seeks to rejoin. To the soul, change represents the most direct route to expand beyond the limits presented by a fearful personality.

The ego was given the function of keeping self safe until the age of reason. It is at that point that you are aware of clear inner messages and you have the ability to interpret these messages and ultimately choose your actions accordingly. Many of you, however, have reached well beyond the age of reason and still do you allow yourselves to be dictated to by the parental ego, seeing yourselves as powerless children.

It is always your choice. The path without change, the limited way of the ego, will give your body the message that life is not unlimited and that it is dangerous to live fully.

Ultimately these messages will cause the body to begin to turn away from life through disease and aging.

If, however, you begin to listen to the soul – speaking to you through the sounds of intuition and the insights of imagination – your life will be extraordinary. You will begin to reflect the view of yourself as dynamic, creative, ongoing movement and energy. The ultimate message to the body then will be that life is good and meant to be experienced fully and that the body should choose more and more of life.

Do you want to know how to make your life less traumatic and more understandable? Listen, simply listen to those inner stirrings and promptings your ego would have you disregard. In this way will you begin to make the choices that will end your need to create catastrophe in your life so that you will be physically forced to listen.

You, more than any other creatures we have known, have devised the most creative and ingenious ways of effecting growth without appearing to have done so. You will go to any length so that you might take no responsibility or control for the situation that forces you to move and grow – from accidents involving physical injuries, to being fired from jobs that are no longer appropriate, to being robbed of possessions that are in truth burdens, to being abandoned by friends so that you might make space for new ones.

All of this drama, simply to appease an ego so afraid of initiating movement on its own that it would prefer to deal with trauma rather than experience the unknown.

Change, the most fearful of words to the ego, is what all things upon the earth plane do. Change is a constant, a given. The process of change is your closest connection to the creative unlimited energy of the divine.

Your concept of God is quite strange. You believe God to be perfect, but if something is perfect it is finished, the standard is set, it is complete, absolute, and limited. Is that concept not also the one

89

you have of death? The energy we know as God is ongoing, totally alive, ever moving, expanding, and growing – it is dynamic and creative and, beloved, changing constantly.

The more your life reflects those God-like qualities, the more you move within the divine's conscious stream of light and power. Bless those situations that impose the greatest difficulty. You have caused them so you might no longer experience a drain on your life force.

You have caused it all. You have used your power to remove people from your life, to create "accidents" that "just happen." Robberies are not random chance, illnesses are not punishments from a God who does not love you. You create it all.

None of this need occur in your life if you listen and act from an open heart that expresses the desires of the deep self. Listen, trust, act in accordance with what you feel inside – even if other does not understand your way.

There are four levels of understanding upon the earth plane. On the first level you look at each situation in your life from a perspective of irresponsibility – you feel always acted upon from without, you blame and hold guilty those around you, always other is the cause of your difficulties. Life at this level is full of anger and resentment.

On the next level you reluctantly take some responsibility, you may still hold other guilty and project blame, but you now look toward forgiveness as a way to absolve the pain.

For in forgiveness you know that you will be released from the grip of resentment – a most dangerous emotion if held within your body.

Then there will come a time when you become accountable for all that occurs within the life you create. You see clearly that there is no one to blame or make to feel guilty, no one at fault. Where could you place blame, if you were to understand that events in your life merely reflect your deep self attempting to move and make itself heard? It is at this point that you know that forgiveness of other is not even an issue, that the only one you need forgive is self for not acting consciously when the call was first heard.

We shall call the fourth and final step toward your understanding mastery. It is on this level that you understand with absolute clarity and sensitivity how important it is that the stirrings of the spirit not go unheeded. At this point upon your path you follow your heart, allowing yourself to be moved to action by the Source and living from the center of your being. There is no hesitancy in actions that flow with ease from your recognition of the need to heed each message communicated from the deep self.

This mastery dwells within and is available to all. You have held this master's hand during those times when you lived your life from a point of cause rather than from reaction to the mindless motion of the outer world.

Learn to hear this master in the whispers of your soul seeking change.

# Focus on Change

In order to locate on which of the four levels of understanding you are currently working answer the following questions to see where you most comfortably fit.

1. Do you feel victimized or acted upon by the world? Are you angry at the way your life has worked out? Do you often feel resentful and cheated by circumstances? Do you feel others are at fault if your needs are unmet? Do you believe that money is the primary means to meeting your needs and making you happy?

2. Do your feelings get hurt easily? Do you try to give others the "benefit of the doubt" by rationalizing or forgiving them, but deep down you still feel hurt? Are you sometimes surprised how certain situations turn out? Are your expectations unrealized? Do you rationalize and try to forgive behaviour of others, but in your heart you still feel hurt? Do you believe money is a means to an end? Do you use the lack of money as an excuse for not doing things?

3. Do you see the synchronicity surrounding you everywhere in the world? Regardless of the results are you totally accountable? Are you more interesting in learning from another's perspective then in persuading them to yours? If things do not work according to your expectations do you look for the lesson? Do you believe that if you do what you love the money will follow? Do you think money is energy?

4. Do you trust unconditionally, without any attempt whatsoever to alter or manipulate your experience? Do you thank God for the bad as well as the good and mean it knowing there is no good or bad only wholeness? Do you consciously cultivate the internal "witness" preferring to honor the sacredness of any experience, rather than being an active participant in

influencing its outcome? Do you refuse to allow others to motivate you through guilt. Do you follow your intuition implicitly? Do you engage in your livelihood as a creative expression regardless of the monetary reward? Are there other means of payment which are more important than money to you? Is your security found only in the Source?

Each question in each of the four levels represents where and on what terms you are living your life. There are no wrong answers or lessor levels, only impartial information for you on how well you are currently being served by a particular perception you may hold . As you expand your consciousness you continue to grow naturally towards a higher realization of how life is living through you. As you become more Unbound, you are able to reach for the next stage of your development.

# The Giveaway: A Process to Witness Who You Are

*"You are the original giveaway. Through
the miracle of divine creation you were
formed by the vibration of love and light.
The Source then presented you with the
ultimate gift of free will, allowing you to
begin your search for self."*

$\mathrm{A}$llowing Transition to come into your life brings you closer to the Divine. You are magnificently alive and totally present during this stage called Transition as you free fall toward Transformation. To assist you we offer the opportunity to take part in a giveaway of closure so that you might bid farewell to an event or creation in your life.

Many of the burdens experienced in your life are due to your lengthy attachments to your creations. Once you create, it is essential that you consciously, purposely release yourself from the responsibility of ownership.

As co-creator with the Divine you receive your greatest pleasure and joy from the ability you share with God – making your love of self visible through the act of creation.

It is the world that would have you believe there is joy in possession. Creation is light, possession is heavy.

Your essence will have a remembrance of the power of a giveaway for it signifies ultimate freedom for both the creator and its creation. You are the original giveaway.

Through the miracle of divine creation you were formed by the vibration of love and light. The Source then presented you with the ultimate gift of free will, allowing you to begin your search for self.

In the final stages of Tradition, you were asked to "let go" of, "to leave behind", "to abandon," and "give up." It was in this way that your free will released you into the void of the unknown called Transition. You will be renewed and reborn during this stage of gestation.

Your exiting from the security known as Tradition has with it a feeling of resignation. Often you are resigned to the need to give up and to let go, not out of joyous abandon, but rather as a final gasp. Your departure from Tradition is not always conscious nor a welcome change.

Regardless of whether the events that carry you away from Tradition are conscious or unconscious, we ask that they be fully blessed and recognized as a superb vehicle for your deliverance. There will come a time, however, during Transition that you must go beyond what might have been perceived by your mind as mere coincidence, random circumstances, or preordained fate.

By this we mean that you must step out in faith in such a way as to prepare yourself consciously for the next stage. Yet in Transition you are asked to BE STILL, DO NOTHING, HAVE FAITH. Give away through non-action.

It is time during Transition to clear a space for your vision of Transformation to reveal itself. It is already within you, you must only allow it to come forth. So it is that you are now asked to purposefully, intentionally, willingly participate in a giveaway – to give away those things that are blocks to the light that illuminates your vision and shows you the way home. Give away your addictions, your habits, your dependencies.

A giveaway is a deliberate, conscious release through no action. There is nothing to do, only refrain from doing. Discontinue doing those things that block your connection with the light. Give away those things that are loved for their momentary pleasure, but ultimately bring you suffering.

Give away all things foreign to your essence and toxic to your nature. Give away those things that deny you your divine destiny. Give away your dependency on external substances, give away your need for approval, give away your addiction to control and manipulate.

In order to have these dependencies in your life you are required to do something, for each of them takes life energy to maintain. We ask that you give away your need to do something.

Instead find new balance and harmony by doing nothing. It is your nature to be without dependencies, without chemicals, without toxins and poisons.

In Tradition, you were asked to give up, to abandon those things that represented the greatest security to the mind, in order to experience your greatest freedom. Your mind perceived this simple exchange as one of great sacrifice. Yet it is the very concept of sacrifice that must now be left firmly behind in the worn beliefs of Tradition. We ask that you replace sacrifice with a joyous giveaway.

In Tradition you are preoccupied with what you see others giving to you. Your total attention is focused exclusively on what you might "get." You conspire with the world to define your own worth and value based on the things other might give you. You have been dependent and needy.

It is a belief held by the world that what you need others have. You believe that you are given your jobs, salaries, education, promotions, even, beloved, love. Always, while concerned with the act of taking will you get less than you truly deserve.

You let the world control you through your need to receive from it. If it is your belief that the world has what you need, then you will initiate the most elaborate creative endeavors imaginable in order to get it. These schemes are responsible for what you call the evils of the world. You believe that another has what you need and so you devise a way to get it.

Look again and choose a new focus in a different direction. It is what you give to the world, not what you receive from it that makes you happy. That which you joyously give tells much more about who you believe yourself to be than what is given to you.

To give willingly to the world places a new dimension within the realm you call reality. Give away your talents, give away your creativity, give away your abundance, give away your love – give away yourself, beloved, so that you might witness the truth of who you really are.

It is not difficult for you to let go and abandon those things found in Tradition although you pretend it to be so. It is not difficult to let go of anger, depression, fear, to give up pain, disease, and death. Who amongst you would not wish to release yourselves from this misery?

Yet what of those subtle limitations that disguise themselves as friends and seduce you into their habitual cycle? What of those things that you believe support your very life, those things without which life seems less than tolerable – what of your dependencies?

A giveaway is an offering believed to be of value that concludes one stage and signifies a readiness to receive another. A giveaway in its undoing will send a message deep into your psyche that shall prepare the way for a different destination.

Give away that which holds great value in its addictive qualities to the ego. Give away that which you believe you could never do without. Separate yourself from your habits and your addictions, so that you might join yourself once again with the Source. Go toward your greatest fear for within it will be found the greatest light.

Your giveaway will set you free to soar. The light has never abandoned you, your vision never left. But you have not seen clearly for your sight has been blinded by the garish lights of the outer world and dulled by its belief in limitation and scarcity. It is your destiny to facilitate, through the raising of your vibration, the coming New Age. Go toward the light within and see clearly your own glory.

Give away what your ego holds dear. Give away your pattern of failure so that you might behold your own success. Give away your dependency upon foreign substances, so you might reclaim your independence from limitation. Give away your addictive need to manipulate and control, so that you might restore your own childlike spontaneity.

Give away your habits, vices, and grievances that diffuse and cloud your light. The clear space they leave behind within you will help you to remember the bargain you made with self so long ago, and how much was in truth given away at that time.

# Focus on Giveaway

A giveaway is a Native American custom used to give gifts to a group. You may use it, however, as a symbol of your willingness to release and unburden yourself. Write down the areas in your life that you would like to attract new energy, new experiences, new beliefs or possessions.

Now list those things in your life you believe limit you. Write down the most simple thing first, such as cleaning out your closets, or giving up coffee, then your most difficult – perhaps giving up an addictive relationship. Then place your lists side by side and see where your two lists coincide. It is at this intersection that you need to focus your attention.

Because you are in Transition it is still important to realize that there is no major motion necessary. So a giveaway is an act of ritual performance. It is more like abstaining from, rather than struggling to rid yourself of something. Do not pretend; if you are not ready to release do not say you are.

There is energy available in Transition for you to let go of those things that do not support you. You will gain a new sense of your own integrity as you bring into balance those things in your life that lessen who you really are.

# Give Away Dependency

*"Overcome only one illusion – that what you need will be found outside of self and by so doing begin to master all others."*

The many forms of dependency attest to your highly creative nature, for in reality all forms of dependence or addictions originate from only one illusion – that you are in need of something outside of self. Unfortunately, it is only when you grow weary of the endless, unsatisfying, and hopeless search to find meaning and value outside of self that you will even attempt to give up dependency and seek to find your truth where it has always been – within.

You are dependent on others for feelings of approval, you are dependent upon stimulants to make you feel better, you are dependent upon external status to remind you who you are, you are dependent on relationships to make you feel loved. You are quite literally addicted to the view that what you want lies outside of yourself. It is a dangerous game that has created the world you now witness.

What is called for now is to proclaim your own independence and to become fearless masters who seek and find their answers and truth from within themselves. To become such a master it may be necessary for you to pass through, as quickly as you can, the interdependence found in groups, where each piece of the whole can become healed.

Mastery, freedom, enlightenment, expansion are all ways of saying the same thing – ISNESS. ISNESS is the all encompassing present moment and your full participation in it. Anything that takes you away from that consciousness disrupts your connection. Acceptance, surrender, allowance are the means provided so that you might receive ISNESS. Overcome only one illusion – that what you need will be found outside of self and by doing begin to master all others.

You have created monsters outside yourself called compulsions. You even believe that they control you, that without them you would not survive. In truth you have dominion over all things upon this earth – physical as well as mental. Rid yourself of these obsessions that leach life from you.

You feel no true joy while doing the bidding of your addictions; it is rather the fear experienced in not doing that keeps you addicted. Whatever you believe yourself to be dependent upon, it is now time to experience yourself differently.

You believe that something is required from you when you are asked to refrain. Immediately your mind moves into denial and justification. Yet your hearts know that you have given pieces of your self-esteem as payment for what is ultimately your destruction. Know that we ask nothing from you and instead bring the gift of strength and wholeness to you through group energy.

Give away your need to feel less. Go within and listen to the still small voice that asks you to do nothing. Then listen to the voice of addiction in the mind, justifying your need to sacrifice. Do nothing. Do nothing that does not make you more of the unlimited god you are. You need nothing for you are all. Find yourself as you give away your dependency.

This is a difficult subject and will not meet with unanimous approval. Fortunately, we are no longer dependent on other's approval for our identity. We state the truth as we know it. As always you may do with this communication as you wish.

Clearly, the earth is a ground upon which you are given the opportunity to achieve mastery over all illusions and regain your understanding of who you are and remember the purpose for which you have come to this plane. Prepare a space within your being now in order to receive this wisdom by simply abstaining from those things that depress your spirit. You are loved for your courage and for your willingness to begin giving away those things that harm you.

# Focus on Dependency

When we are caught in our false or addictive nature we have become out of balance with our Being. Peace is attained through being rather than doing. You can not go out and "get" peace because it comes naturally in repose. Restoration of our being is achieved through refraining. Action and energy are necessary in order to continue any of our addictions. To eliminate an addiction takes doing nothing.

Our addictions in the beginning are attempts on our part to make a situation more tolerable. Instead of dealing with a situation straight on, we find ways to deny or dilute it.

Identify where or what in your life is an unhealthy dependency. Do you work, drink, eat, gamble, spend or drug excessively? Are you addicted to approval?

For one day DO NOTHING in order to make a difficult situation easier. Do not take a bite, pick up a drink, do more work, make a phone call or run away from IT. Instead, at times of stress, sit still, be silent and experience your desired dependency; listen to it call to you but do not respond. You don't have to give it away for ever, but just for today Do Nothing So You Might Learn Something.

Experience the feelings from not feeding your dependencies. Draw them out, or write them down if you want. Begin to see the energy it takes to continue this behaviour. In order to lose weight, stop drinking or drugging, get over obsessive relationships, or stop compulsively working, you need to Do Nothing, but welcome and nurture the freedom that will follow.

# Give Away Control

*"It is through your obsession with order
and control that you repress your own life
energy and thus literally deny yourself
with your ultimate controlling mechanism
– death."*

The reason you experience so much difficulty in your life is that you struggle and fight against the chaos from which your essence naturally springs. It is in your reluctance to give up control that you resist the peace that comes from surrender. Yet it is actually your fear of chaos that controls you.

Your unwillingness to allow the natural flow to direct itself brings resistance to your life force. The chaos you feel would result if you became less controlling is actually only the life force within you attempting to unify itself once again with the inevitable force of creation. What the mind believes to be chaos is actually creativity in action.

You are part of creation and as such you are most beautiful, most wondrous, most magnificent, and most precious. These are the qualities that make up the ongoing creation that because of your fears appears as chaos. For you to merge with the energy of creation you must only allow it to fill you; stand still long enough and it will begin to seep into your waking and sleeping moments.

You have each manipulated your relationships, your environments, your experiences in order to force a particular outcome judged by the mind to be superior. In reality, your meddling only retards the natural rhythm of the Source attempting to reunite itself with you. Your need to control all the situations in your life keeps you separate and alone.

What you call chaos is actually a beautiful spiral song known by the ancient wisdom of your soul. The unknown holds within it the promise of everything that is meaningful and real. Through your obsession with order and control, you repress your own life energy and thus literally deny yourself through your ultimate controlling mechanism – death. Try as you may you will never hold back the primal force that causes change and alters creation. If you try, your expended efforts will only consume your very life force.

Why would anyone prefer predictability to randomness, stagnation to invention, boredom to excitement? The known has delivered to you all that it contains, but the unknown holds the promise of what might become.

The perfection known as God fits none of your definitions of orderliness or absolutes. Perhaps you have difficulty finding God because of your own descriptions and expectations.

Place less attention on controlling your own unlimited nature by living with a deeper sense of discipline. Listen and move when the source that resides within you says with love and honor – "move in this way, move now."

To be truly disciplined is to become a disciple of the light. To be disciplined means to be courageous and hold steadfastly to your inner knowingness, regardless of the response given by the world.

Most of you need more freedom, more chaos, more spontaneity, more laughter, more delight in your day. You are stern taskmasters and harsh disciplinarians. We ask only that you be true masters and loyal disciples to self and the unfolding moment.

105

The truth that is yours is not some stagnate, unchanging body of information known thousands of years ago and frozen for all time. It is instead a truth that is being shown to you during each glorious moment of your life, a wisdom that shall be found only in your willingness to embrace fully each day of life that is yours – moment by moment.

Be still; listen for the inner sounds. Be disciplined. Disregard your plans and expectations and free fall into the spontaneous moment and you will be rewarded with a life lived out of the intention to live. What else might you want, – for those who intend to live shall never die.

Go today and live with determination and discipline knowing, in truth, you cannot know what to do this moment for the next. Be afraid of nothing that the future holds for you and that the Source asks of you. Follow your still small voice into the next moment and then the next and then the next and then the next and when you look back you will see only a string of pearls so wondrous that you will cry with joy over their creation.

Life is a living canvas; it cannot be made to your orders, planned, nor contained. Instead it is continuous, ongoing, dynamic, fragile in its appearance, but resilient and indestructible in its reality.

You who have in the past attempted to limit the unlimited, to organize the spontaneous, will forever live in the terror of losing control. We ask that you give away that which in truth you never had so you might free yourself from the illusion of control.

# Focus on Control

W e often expend much of our energy attempting to control other people and the events in our lives. This can be very frustrating because we actually have very little control over certain situations. The paradox is that the more we try to control others the less influence we have with them.

See control as a continuum:

A little  A lot

Now ask yourself where on this line do the actions of others lie? Can you really control another person's attitudes, or their actions? No, of course not. Who is it that you have most control over? Yourself, of course. Even if you don't always have control over the situations in your life, you always have control over how you will respond to them.

When relating to others, it works well to give them a greater sense of their freedom of choice so you are not in a power struggle. This opens up a dialogue that establishes mutual respect and allows you more influence in their decision making process. This is not a ploy, or a tactic, but an authentic way of inter acting. You might say something like "I don't know what your decision will be? After all you are your own person. But, I can tell you from my experience this is what I'd do?" Remember, though when you release control you must be willing to live with the results of the other persons decision.

Answer the following questions. Then allow yourself to relinquish the illusion of control so that you might establish a sense of real serenity.

## *Control Questionnaire*

1. What are you most afraid would happen if you were unable to control the outcome of situations in your life?

2. How much energy do you expend on manipulating results in your life?

3. What would it feel like to let go and know that things are proceeding perfectly. Imagine how liberating this might be.

4. Do you really have control over this situation or this person? What do you have control over?

# The Harvest: Gathering The Seeds of Your Truth

*"Within the ripened fruit is a new
seed that shall perpetuate and facilitate
growth. The seed that is planted matures
and Transformation is its yield."*

In giving away what was believed by the mind to be of value, you have enlarged your vision. To travel the Cycle of Ascendancy you must give up those things from Tradition that no longer serve you. In Transition you become still so that you might receive your vision. In Transformation you acknowledge the part you play in the metamorphosis of the world.

Transition is a time of assessing and discovery-discovering your own destiny and assessing your alternatives. You are asked to make little outer movement during this stage, yet we assure you the shifts will be profound. Proceed slowly in Transition in order to allow for a natural evolution.

What of those things found in Tradition that still hold within them positive aspects of the light? Transition shall provide you with the time and the clarity necessary to assess.

When you are still you are able to discern those things that are worthless and should be discarded and those things that hold value and should be reclaimed.

To reclaim is another word for the harvest. There is sufficient time in Transition to harvest those things of Tradition that still serve you.

The three essential aspects of Transition are:

*The Giveaway* – a conscious clearing of space through the removal of what is unessential. The giveaway is symbolized by the burning of the fallen leaf.

*The Harvest* – a gathering and joining together, in a new form, those elements that remain vital. The harvest is symbolized by tying the autumn leaf back onto the tree.

*The Thaw* – the surrendering of all life back into the unity of oneness. The thaw is symbolized by the seed of desire returning to the earth.

In Transformation the seed begins to germinate – along with the dream of the tiller that it might grow and bear fruit. The purpose of the planting shall be to produce yield, for in that yield shall be found the seed of the future. Yet to everything there is a season, and the yield must be harvested or else wither upon the vine. Clearly there is a time when the cause is less essential than its result.

Extract what is nourishing, abandon what remains. Tradition always yields you a rich bounty, yet if you stay too long upon its vine your efforts will begin to sour and decay. Timing is essential in your world.

It is time now to harvest all the rich experiences found in Tradition that may still hold within them a grain of truth. From this truth shall we create joyful nourishment. Gather together the many in order to sustain the one. Join together the fragments of the self for the purpose of unifying and strengthening the whole.

Within the ripened fruit are the seeds that shall perpetuate and facilitate rebirth. The seed that is planted matures and Transformation is the fruit of your labour.

The cycle of the soil is merely a metaphor of your own soul. The hope of eternal life is found in the fruit of the labour. Within your free expression and creativity is found the seed of eternal growth and rebirth.

Harvest the good that has come from Tradition and from your experiences therein. Know that your experiences have matured in Transition and that it is indeed time for you to yield yourself unto yourself and so reap the benefits. Take pride in and credit for all that has gone before, so that you might look forward to all that is yet to be.

Your positive experiences contain within them the seeds of your new one. Yet remember, it is a law that you may produce nothing better in the future than is currently contained within the seed of your present. So it is that the cycle is ever evolving and expanding. What germinates as Transformation in the future, is created as a hybrid within this moment as you assess Tradition in Transition.

Look favorably therefore upon all the experiences produced within Tradition and the value they hold. Know that what you are willing to harvest now with an open heart shall yield you in the future a loving crop. That is the Cycle known as Ascendancy – each planting perfecting itself through its future seed.

Your willingness at this time to harvest and enjoy the fruits of your own labour will enable your spirit to feed itself throughout Transition. It is in this way that you shall sustain and nurture yourself by your own hand.

You are powerful, resourceful, wise, and true, yet often you are unable to feel your own validity because you keep yourself fragmented and alone. The shaft of wheat holds many individual kernels, yet when the grain is milled together it combines to produce what you call the staff of life. In the past you have refused the

111

gift of healing found within the harvest. Gather now the pieces of your own psyche together so you may experience the nourishment found in the wholeness of your soul.

There are experiences and understandings received during Tradition that will aid you during the harvest. They have their origin in Tradition, yet if you but alter your perception of them slightly they will render you a new view. They are; continuous time, cause and effect, the purpose of the physical body.

It is a traditional view, widely held, that the events that occur in the outer world are random, accidental, chance, or coincidence. It would serve your future Transformation if you begin while in Transition to understand that God makes no mistakes. And although you believe to err is human, beloved, in truth you are divine and as such incapable of error too.

The mind has convinced you that the world you see outside of self is not to be trusted, for it is believed to be highly unpredictable and extremely erratic in its occurrences. Know that the circumstances and events that make up your experiences are mathematically precise, coldly calculated, and perfectly logical.

These are, however, the very characteristics the mind loves to use to identify itself – rational, predictable, logical. It is again a matter of projection. The mind has taken on the attributes of the universe and conveniently projected the evidence of who you truly are out onto the universe.

It is little wonder that you are constantly surprised by the responses received in the outer world. You often feel quite terrified of what is to come. In your attempts to ward off impending disaster you manipulate your environment so that it might give you the desired response. You have, however, been attempting to fix what is not broken. No longer hold the outer world responsible for what you experience.

Rail against the universe no more, for your problem cannot be found out there, so naturally, neither can your solution. Instead look within for both – you are all of it, beloved, the good, the bad, the cause, the effect, the question, and the answer. Your balance is to be found within these polarities.

It is you who pull to you, by virtue of your own electrical magnetic impulses, the events in your life. Those impulses are comprised of the collective vibration registered as your emotions, beliefs, attitudes, thoughts, words, and deeds. The environment in which you find yourself simply conforms to and mirrors back the raw material you have presented it. The world outside holds no action in it. Man is the only actor upon this stage called earth and with every thought he puts into play thousands of possibilities that at some time become his experience.

Those thousands of experiences will reappear at appropriate times in your life in order to provide you with the various lessons needed. You, in your impeccable, unlimited design, have been given dominion over all things upon this plane. Dominion is found within the impact of your decisions, choices, and opportunities while exhibiting here on earth.

In the past you have believed it possible to be cast out of Eden by a God who was displeased by your actions. This is a lie conjured up by the ego and perpetuated in order to keep you weak and fearful. It has been from this deficiency within your psyche that you have been forced to create your reality.

Behold the world around you, beloved, and see clearly how it represents a view that God is vengeful and man is evil.

You are not bad, God is not punitive, and We who hover now around your plane only attempt to arouse you from your unconscious sleep through the stirring of new breezes of which these messages are a part.

It is time to bring your sense of self in alignment with the truth found in all of creation – you are no accident, life is not random, there could never be a mistake. There are simply choices and consequences devoid of judgment. You have for too long now asked that the world give you things that it is incapable of giving. It is this traditional view that is the cause of much of your misery. Look no longer to the world for your salvation.

You are so grand that you need fear nothing on this planet. There is no problem that you cannot solve, and even more precisely, there is no problem that you have not created for the purpose of learning. It is instead time to focus on the tools given for the purpose of Transformation. Everything is here to help you. Look at the symbols and projections you experience. They are here for your benefit.

The universe provides you with the most elaborate set of road maps called your experiences from which you may be directed home. There is nothing that needs to be manipulated or fixed for everything is already proceeding perfectly. It is only your view of things which needs correcting, your faith that needs fixing.

Exchange the traditional view of the world for one of Transformation. Within your perception lies reality. Reverse the. view you have of yourself, with the role you so willingly give up to the world. The world is forever static, precise, dependable, predictable, fixed, and logical. You, however, are radiant, imaginative, expressive, impetuous, totally alive, undulating creative energy. You are the cause and the world is your effect.

Pretend to be powerless no more. Cause to create from a deep abiding sense of inner worth, so that your effects become worthy of you. See yourself correctly within the equation of life that begins with you. If you continue to refuse your responsibility in this chain of life, it may also end with you. Change your thought patterns so you may surround yourself with new energy and choose a different reality.

It is also your traditional approach to continuous time that keeps you from harvesting its real value. Time only appears to the mind to be continuous. In truth, time occurs in a stop-and-go freeze frame effect, much like the stop action of your cameras. Action occurs, time is momentarily halted allowing the effect of that action to release itself into other dimensions and then resumes once again.

The purpose of this stop-and-start process you call time is to create an opportunity for the causes as well as their effects to disengage from the earth's atmosphere and to connect themselves into pre-existing accumulated responses. This rendezvous between cause and effect may be achieved only if time is somehow altered.

The freeze frame effect makes it possible for you then to choose which of the results, created from your past actions, you wish to have re-enter into your current experience for the purpose of instruction.

Thoughts of like intensity and feelings attract each other and form groups of similar thoughts. If seen from inner space where they collect they would look quite like the atoms and molecules that make up all of your solid matter and in this way thoughts are things.

These molecular structures attach themselves one to another until the thought pattern established is substantial enough to be identified through its movement and vibration – what you refer to as motivation. This structure may float around just outside of your perception of time and space awaiting the opportunity to be recalled by you as a particular result.

We ask that you begin to look at time in a new way so that it might instruct you accordingly. Time is not continuous; it can be easily manipulated by you through your thoughts. Thoughts, words, and deeds are not held within time, so they provide you with an easy access to other dimensions.

Thoughts, words, and deeds must be released away from the

present or there would be an implosion from the interaction. Elsewhere in the Cosmos, sophisticated energy forms manifest instantaneously. They understand perfectly the balance between cause and effect. By comparison, your concept of continuous time is interminable.

Manifestation is dependent upon the clarity of intention and the intensity of thought called desire. Limiting beliefs alter the precise definition of your accumulated thought pattern. It is for this reason that you may wish and pray for an impending result, yet sabotage the outcome through conflicting attitudes and opinions. From this you may clearly see that both beliefs and thoughts form your experience, rather than the traditional view.

In order to manipulate time to your best advantage, watch each thought as it grows within your mind and then follow it out through the cracks found within the space of your day.

Those of you who practice meditation have experienced this method of time alteration. It is at those times during your meditation when you are most furiously attempting to "get out of your mind," watching your thoughts as they arise, only to be replaced by the next – –. that your experience of time is impossibly long and drawn out.

If, on the other hand, you have no expectation, try to "get nowhere," your thoughts leave and arrive with no notice and your experience of time is one of swift flight.

If you wish to slow time, you must only stay with your thoughts consciously. Ask of your thoughts from where they have come and before they have been summarily dismissed follow them out to where they go. Proceed with caution, however, for you can easily be pulled outside of the veil of forgetfulness and have an experience of total past life recall.

Many are the number of those who unconsciously allow themselves to be pulled into the past or mindlessly into the future and so never remain present in order to create their own reality.

You can alter time with your consciousness; you have dominion over all things upon this plane, tangible as well as intangible. There are great benefits for your being able to do so. If you are able to expand and contract what you have traditionally believed to be the inflexible boundaries of time, you will begin to expand your belief in the unlimitedness of your own boundaries.

The most essential benefit is that you will remain awake during the actual process you call thinking. As you begin to pay more attention to the process of forming thoughts, so will you become more selective in their dispensing.

If you could but see the amazing thoughts that emanate from your mind – those that, by law, must return with a result, you would think twice about what you allow into your minds and out of your mouths. Each thought must travel outward in order to collect and attract to itself other thought forms of similar vibration.

Your thought patterns then hover as a shroud around the earth waiting to be recalled by you as an appropriate response to your future thought or action.

The thought pattern of collected energies used in the expression in the molecular structure of the verb to hate appears as

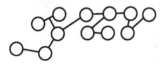

When this molecule has collected sufficient power and density it will then insist upon a means of expression called a consequence.

The thought pattern of the collected energies used in the expression of love is ●

The molecular structure for the truth contained in love is infinitely more simple, much less complex and convoluted. It is your mind that fights the simplicity of the answer called love, for the mind finds value in difficulty. As love grows, it expresses itself by expanding from the inside out. It never breaks its own circle nor needs to add to itself from the outside.

Whenever your thoughts choose love over fear, peace over violence, pleasure over pain, light over darkness, life over death, you are in service to all humanity. For by so doing you disengage one component of the complexity of hate as you simultaneously contribute to the growth of love. Truth shall always triumph over the illusions of limitation.

When you are able to remain consciously within each new thought as it arises you will be led to the place where time stands still and God waits. Choose well which thoughts you wish to feed into the atmosphere today, for each thought contains within it the seed of what you will harvest as your experience tomorrow.

# *Focus on Harvesting*

Balance is what we seek. If you consciously choose to give away things that no longer support your view of yourself, then you must also consciously choose to reclaim those things that are already in place in your life that tend to uplift you.

List those things that were produced within the soil of Tradition, but that still hold benefit for you. Perhaps it is a relationship, or the way you handle your finances; maybe it is your approach to health, or the way you look at your body. Whatever it is, it needs to be consciously appreciated and brought with you into this next stage of your life.

After you have made your list of things that assist you, then do one thing to reinforce your conscious decision to invite them with you into Transformation. If it is a relationship, you might want to call the person and give away your gratitude by affirming what they mean to you in your life. If it is the way you treat your body, then you could give away praise by getting a massage. Do anything that demonstrates your willingness to harvest their fruit during Transformation.

# Body and Spirit

*"Love the one thing to which you
are truly connected at this precise
moment. How can you hope to find your
connection between God and self if you
place no value upon the body that holds
you both together."*

The true purpose of the body is to lead the way, upon this plane of mass, so that the spirit might experience and enjoy. Let it be known that upon this planet of polarities there shall always be two purposes, a mundane one as well as an extraordinary one. It is then your choice as to which you will give your attention.

Your soul has chosen this embodiment over infinite other possibilities and as such your lifetime should not be looked on merely as an accident of birth. Instead, receive huge rewards from your allegiance to and alignment with the body you presently occupy.

Your body is the vehicle through which your spirit will be transported to a new level of understanding this lifetime. It is imperative that you consciously recognize and willingly acknowledge the powerful process in which you are involved so that you might receive its ultimate benefits.

Your body is a sensitive instrument, a wondrous mechanism, designed for the purpose of recording all the various levels of life. These levels of life are what you conceive of as your many and varied experiences. The physical body allows impressions to be made upon her, at the same time that the soul stores the emotional content through vibration. So then these experiences contain within them the potential to alter your moment to moment responses during the current lifetime, as well as your total collective understandings of past lifetimes.

So marvelous are the workings of your body, that scientists have only a minuscule knowledge of what it is truly capable of. You have within you at this moment all the combined attributes of every human who has ever come to this plane before you, as well as all the potential of those who have yet to come. Your body is ready to relinquish all this potential into your experience if you but believe in her possibilities.

Yet you may deny your dreams through the use of limiting beliefs – and you do it all the time. These limiting beliefs will be evidenced as accurate renderings upon your body.

The body is incapable of lying to you. She may, however, be lied to. We refer, of course, to self-deceiving directives given by the limited mind onto a receptive body. Thus what the body is told repeatedly and with intensity eventually is accepted as reality.

The body is an invaluable tool when used as an illustrator of your predominant beliefs. If you wish to witness which is the dominant force in your life, your spirit or your mind, simply look into your mirror. Although it is usually beyond your observation, your body is continuously involved in a form of communicating with your spirit. The messages relayed from one to the other may be seen through the process that you call health or illness and you are both its recipient and creator.

Remember, it is always the soul that has a desire to move, to experience fully all that life offers. Quite literally, it is the soul that has a thirst for life that you, with your choices and beliefs, either quench or stifle. It is the body's purpose to out picture the unseen mystical desires of the spirit so that you will recognize spirit's request. Instead of seeing the underlying truth, however, you drown your body in strong drink and burden it with too much food, becoming unable to sense the sounds of spirit.

The more gluttonous the body the more starved the soul. When the spirit is allowed full movement, the body seems to live on air. When the body receives proper physical nourishment, a communication of love is received in the soul that equates with nurturing. Nourishment for the body and nurturing for the soul are translated as a cherishing of life. Repression and denial of either translates as disease and death.

There are no mysteries – except for those who refuse to see. All the clues are there within clear sight so that you might discover your own destiny. See the simplicity in all things rather than the complexities the mind would prefer.

The body shall be the last battleground upon which you practice your games of war and deceit. When you live at peace and unity within your own body, you will surrender to a new understanding that will facilitate a higher vibration. This vibration shall identify you to those of your ascended group for the purpose of remembering. If your body is unloved it will not reflect the aura of high vibration and you will not be recognized.

In the past, it has been man's way always to search outside and far away from self. So it has been necessary for the body to produce upon its own flesh a portrait of what transpires within. Close your eyes, and listen to the message communicated through the inner workings of your body.

Love the one thing to which you are truly connected at this precise moment. How can you hope to find your connection between self and God if you place no value upon the body that holds you both together?

You cannot transcend this world without taking your body.

122

You are responsible for its creation, for its welfare, for its maintenance, and now finally for transforming the body back into the substance of Light from where it came.

Your body has been a loyal servant and you must now love her sufficiently to take her with you on your ascension. You have all abused the body and then simply discarded the evidence through death – lifetime after lifetime leaving the body, attempting to transcend with only the spirit. When you abandon your body, beloved, you leave behind an essential part of your own soul essence. It is then necessary for you to reincarnate and Remember.

You are destructively attached to the illusions you have created around the body – the dwellings, the clothing, the games of lust and love. You have attempted to mold the body into a form specified by another. But none of you have known the pure wonder of acceptance of the body as it expresses as the divine reflection of who you truly are.

You have for too long separated the soul from the body, giving to one at the expense of the other. Balance is always the answer. Understand that when you trust your inner self, the outer one will function perfectly and both will be united in wholeness. There is the Source, there is the soul, and there is the body – the trinity of truth found upon the earth plane. You can no longer escape this truth and yet remain part of the whole. Fragment your own wholeness no more.

Your final journey on this plane is to devote the body to personal service. Do you not wonder where Jesus' body is, why when he ascended he did not leave it behind to rot and decay? You love your bodies not enough to take them with you onward to your destination. It is time you lighten your bodies through love in preparation for your ultimate journey. Your bodies have become too heavy from the burdens they carry.

There are those who believe that you abuse no one or no thing when abusing your body. This is a serious lie, for you can be no better to other than you be to yourself. Deceive yourself no more. The way is through God, beloved, but your vehicle is the body. Your wholeness is found in the balance between body and soul held together through the divine mind of God known as peace – practice it now.

# Focus on Body and Spirit

It is time to listen to and learn from the beauty of the body. How can we really trust the nature of all things if we rigidly control, manipulate and override our physical body? The body will quite literally bring you back to your senses. Both the body and the spirit exist in present time reality. The mind, however, drags you to a past you cannot change, and into a future you cannot control.

The body's natural instinct will return you to simplicity. For the next seven days refrain from any externally imposed demands made on the body by the limited mind. Instead bring the body back into its own natural balance by letting her BE. During a complete weekend, take time to live in accord with your body's instinctive and healthy nature.

1. Bring the body back to balance through rest. Really rest the body. For one complete weekend give her sufficient sleep. Let her sleep whenever and as much as she might need. Disregard the mind whenever it makes fearful demands on the body. Rest, relax, restore. Resist your addiction to accomplish for just one weekend.

2. After giving the body sufficient rest, place her in the most natural environment possible. The body resonates most effectively with a place in nature. Go to the ocean, walk in the woods, climb a mountain, sit under a tree, lie with your back on the ground and watch the clouds accumulate or study the moon. The vibratory rate of nature will fine tune your physical instrument so that you and the Divine will be in harmony. Draw in the energy through full complete breathes of inspiration.

3. Eat simply; nurture your body. Trust your hunger rather than your appetite. Whenever and whatever your body wants in the way of food allow her to have. Know that one step in

trust will lead to greater overall balance within the totality of your Being.

4.  Water your body. Drink clean clear water and let yourself be purified. When it feels right to you immerse the body in warm water and let her be bathed in the clarity. Cleansing the aura (the energy body that surrounds the physical body) of depression (low density vibrations) is as easy as taking a shower or bath.

# The Thaw: Flowing From Transition Into Transformation

*"Imagine the Source, seeing its own
image in a clear and still pond, recognized
within itself such supreme love that the
pond stirred with movement. Imagine
that movement causing the image in the
pool to ripple, fragment, multiply, and
expand into each of you."*

We welcome all who are poised at the brink of Transformation. Transition never formally ends, instead it simply melts and flows into Transformation.

You, precious pieces of the whole who find it difficult to witness your value, are held together by a thought so profound your language has no means of expression. Can you imagine a thought so powerful that it produces consciousness as an expression of self-love. Can you imagine a thought so loving it produces creation as an expression of joy? This is your heritage, your ancestry.

You are the multiple reflections found within the love of God. Imagine the Source, seeing its own image in a clear and still pond, recognized within itself such supreme love that the pond stirred with movement. Imagine that movement causing the image in the pool to ripple, fragment, multiply, and expand into each of you.

Imagine that you are adrift upon the pond, believing the illusion that you are separate and alone, without focus, without connection to the Source.

That moment is known to you as Creation. As the water now stills itself, you are restored once again as the perfect reflection of the Source. Begin to calm yourself so that the revelation might be reclaimed – you are forever connected to the Source and all aspects of Creation.

What you call the New Age is found in the beginning of Transition – the stilling again of your waters. Transformation shall then occur through your recognition of the reflection you share with God.

The movement created from the light of recognition of the love that was witnessed through the Source is known as the commotion of creation – you believe it to be a big bang. It is now the time of revelation and a return to peace.

When the ripples of the pond have played themselves out, diminish, and no longer give you the illusion of disruption and separation, peace will be restored. In order to return to this natural clarity, there is nothing to do but to allow. The water knows the way; it is by your doing that the confusion continues.

So is it with Transition moving into Transformation – there is nothing to be done, simply an allowance of what is already taking place. We speak to you of a return to innocence, a return to trust, a return to peace. You will remember a time when you shared a common vision as together you presented the perfect reflection of God. Now you indulge the beliefs of those who see themselves as abandoned, broken, and fragmented.

You have an image that your spirit resides within your body, but your body resides within your spirit – once again you have it backwards. Your spirit is the energy field that surrounds your physical body. The spirit of you is so large it could never be contained within the boundaries of mass. Spirit, however, registers itself as the movement within your body, it beats your heart, it moves your limbs and inspires your breath.

Your body is actually frozen thought. You created it through a picture held of how you wished to express. That part of spirit you share as a Co-creator with God is given dominion over certain aspects of its own destiny, one being physical existence.

The thought sent out from spirit lowered itself into light and created your auric impression. Then the light lowered itself into movement that created your mental and emotional vibration. Finally, movement was slowed sufficiently as to create mass that manifested itself as the body. You are spirit, all of you, even that part which is mass and as such is called critical.

You are a physical body, living through grace in a mental/emotional body, living through grace in the light/ auric body, living through grace in the spirit/essential body, living through grace in the cosmic/divine body. You are a cell within the body of the Divine, a particle in the perfection of creation. Without you, wholeness is impossible. No longer deny your divine destination.

There is a sacred space within you that holds within it the memory of who you truly are. In the instant that the Divine looked upon its own reflection and saw you, it stirred through its love of you an individual consciousness as well as the expression of the word Good.

Doubt, fear, failure are not words that hold meaning in God's world. Trust, faith, worth, success, love, and value – these are the words that speak to the spirit.

You hold within your physical body a place where you remember all the goodness of which God spoke. We ask that you enlarge that space within which you have placed your divine memory and your purest vision. It is within you, held behind a wall of frozen tears cried by your soul. Remember the time when you were innocent, pure, and free, when you laughed and cried freely, when you flowed endlessly, when you were the purest expression of love – remember when you were a child.

The world appeared to you as rigid, fixed, and measured. And so you believed that to live therein you too must become frozen. Restore yourself through recalling the splendor of yourself. Allow your sternness to melt into your center of innocence, lay down your imagined burdens and become gentle and calm again, finding the ease and simplicity within.

Do nothing to guard against the truth you hold within.

Instead allow yourself to thaw from the heat stored in the heart that knows the truth. You are a child of God naturally trusting, intimate, and innocent, yet invulnerable.

You cannot harm nor can you be harmed and so you are now free to move in absolute assurance, peace, harmony, and grace.

# Focus on Thawing

Due to the beliefs we formed about the world as children we fear trusting others. If you have difficulty with being vulnerable, trusting, or intimate, begin to see that it is not others you are afraid of but yourself. Entertain the notion that you do not trust yourself, that you are unable to be intimate with you, and feel exposed and vulnerable with yourself.

You can never extend to another person that which you do not give to yourself. Become intimate with your own being, develop your ability to be alone without being lonely. If you cannot be comfortable with yourself you never will be with another person.

Touch your own invulnerability by meditating or reflecting silently on that place within yourself that is absolutely eternal. If you are already meditating, then deepen it by focusing on your invulnerability. It is when you are in this sacred space that you are in connection with an all-knowing part of yourself. It is when you are silent and still that you will feel your absolute strength.

Trust your own divine nature so you might expand and trust your environment. Keep your word, if you say it – then do it no matter what. Your word is law and every time you break it you break a major commitment to yourself. Begin to trust yourself by taking small risks and challenges and not abandoning your position.

Allow the frozen parts of yourself to begin to melt into the wholeness you share with the Source.

# Invulnerability

*"Call out to that part of you held captive*
*behind your wall of frozen fear, so it*
*might hear that you are ready to have the*
*memory of your invulnerability restored."*

During your stay in Transition you have been still, silent, and solicitous to the voice within. From this righteous attitude comes the deep and abiding knowingness that you are invulnerable, harmless, and without guilt. You can not be harmed, nor can you harm another. You are free forever from the endless cycle of pain and guilt.

Invulnerability means without beginning or end, without limit or boundaries, without judgment or condemnation. Try to remember, beloved, the joy that springs from the memory that you are harmless, guiltless, and innocent.

Our job is to awaken within you that memory, to whisper, to cajole, to remind. Your job is to remember, reflect, and restore yourself to the vision you hold within. The salvation of the world rests within your memory – you are essential, powerful, and invulnerable.

Your willingness to release yourself from a tradition built on pain and guilt shall start a chain reaction that creates you as an essential link of freedom for others. You need do nothing for another, you only resolve to remember. Doubt not your part in the restoration of sanity to the world. For doubt is a most destructive weapon used by the mind against your innocence.

Instead have faith that the process of peace is working perfectly. Each morning when you arise, affirm your own indestructibility. Each morning give thanks for your harmlessness, your guiltlessness, your freedom from fear and pain. You can never be hurt, get sick, or die without your own consent.

What would you cause to begin or to complete in your life if you but believed in your own invulnerability? Who would you now be able to love and accept? Where would you venture to go if there were nothing to fear? You would within that instant choose to live a life of impeccability. For if you could but remember that you are invulnerable, without weakness, without a need to defend, then you would give to the world a gift of wholeness and perfection.

Do you not begin to feel a stirring, a melting within your heart that comes from the joy of remembering the truth. For without fear of hurt you can freely love another and without fear of guilt you can freely love self.

Refuse to attack and defend that part of yourself that lies within the heart of God and is beyond your protection. Be assured that the power found within the memory of who you truly are renders you invincible. Drop your shields, your swords, your defenses.

Know that you told yourself the lie that you were weak, unworthy, valueless. You accepted that lie because of your belief in pain and so you pretended to suffer. You accepted the possibility that you could be hurt and the responsibility that you could also hurt. God would not allow such a bargain.

You began to construct an image on the outside, and around your heart a wall of ice so that no one might get close enough to see your imperfection. The wall has only served to keep the lie alive; you are the one denied the vision of beauty and the light hidden behind it. The wall stands as a monument to fear and separation.

Allow the guards you have constructed around your heart to disband. You are strong enough to love and pure enough to trust.

Your heart is eternal and your soul stands within the peaceable kingdom of God.

Call out to that part of you held captive behind your wall of frozen fear, so it might hear that you are ready to have the memory of your invulnerability restored. Allow the greatest possession you have – your real identity – to be restored to your consciousness so you might resume your journey home.

# *Focus on Invulnerability*

Transition is not a stage for struggle, but for surrender. Transition is a time to replace control with consent. Consent to the consciousness that guides all life. This consciousness is within, it is the core Self and you may reach this invulnerable place by being still. Sitting still in meditation allows us to clear away all that is extraneous and creates a space for that part of us which is invulnerable to reveal itself.

1.  Find a comfortable place to sit. Make sure you will not be disturbed for the next 20 minutes.

2.  Allow your body to relax. Use your mind to relax your body mentally; ask each part of your body to relax. Say silently, "My feet are relaxing. My ankles and calves are relaxing." Continue until your whole body surrenders to the feeling of relaxation.

3.  Concentrate on your breath as it comes in and makes contact with the tip of your nostrils. Become a student of the breath; notice every nuance, every sensation that is involved in breathing. Enjoy the process of simply sitting still as you inhale and exhale; feel your connection to life through the inspiration of breath.

4.  Whenever the mind wanders, bring it back to the breath. As a means of concentration you can count your breaths from one to five. Repeat the process over and over. Returning to your breath whenever you find your mind has wandered again.

5.  Finally as you bring your breath into your body follow it down into the core of your being. Find all the places within your body that your breath touches; find that place inside yourself where you abide in peace. Do not doubt it is there. Continue to draw your breath down into your conscious cen-

ter and allow the peace it brings to pour over you. Continue to practice this exercise daily so that you will strengthen your connection and awareness of the invulnerable part of you that can never be harmed and never dies.

# Trust

*"Trust that you hold within a
knowingness that equates with the
rhythm and harmony of all creation."*

The trusting heart holds itself open so it might hear the song sung by the Divine. Trust is a wonderful, freeing, totally expanding tool for transformation. Trust allows you, beloved, to open yourself to all possibilities because you joyfully witness the potential you hold within. Trust is disbelief in doubt.

To trust is to affirm your own perfection. To trust is to acknowledge your own abundance. To trust is to avow your own creative nature. Doubt dispels intuition, imagination, and inspiration. Doubt is a denial and contraction that registers as death to the soul.

Trust that you hold within a knowingness that equates with the rhythm and harmony of all creation. To trust that you possess the vastness of the entire universe within the perfection of one of your cells is to begin to trust that you have come to express upon this planet for a reason and that only through trusting will that reason be made clear.

Placed within your sacred space is your purpose for being. Trust yourself enough to allow it to emerge into consciousness. Trust another enough that they might share your glory. Trust the truth enough to live it without reservation. You cannot make a mis-

137

take if you trust your intuition, your imagination, your still small voice.

In the past, you have mistrusted the movement of your deep self. You have sought your purpose from the mind. It is your heart, not your head, that holds your vision. Do not ask the mind to give you what it does not have.

Trust yourself, have faith in the existence. Doubt nothing that comes from inspiration, deny nothing that comes from imagination, dismiss nothing that comes from intuition.

Trust yourself enough so that you might trust another and together know that you have been entrusted by God to restore the world to peace. Trust and then act with confidence.

# *Focus on Trust*

To cultivate trust you need to let go of control. Trust is the essential element of surrendering to the perfection of the Source. The first step in the process of trust is to simply start small.

1.  For this week do not wear a watch, allowing instead your internal clock to guide you.

2.  Do two things that you would enjoy doing, but that may make you appear foolish.

3.  This weekend schedule absolutely nothing; no errands, or external demands. Instead, trust that you can listen to and be lead by your own internal rhythms. Eat when you are hungry. Sleep when you are tired. Experience the simplicity of your own divine nature. Give yourself the time to be open to the surprises the universe may have in store for you.

If at the end of your day you cannot identify one complete surprise you still have too much scheduled. Trust the Way so that you can open your schedule sufficiently and provide a space big enough to include a surprise. At the end of this day you should be able to say "Wow, I had no idea this morning that I would go here, or do, or see that."

# Intimacy

*"Substance is what you be, Source is what
you have been, and Love is what you are
becoming. This is the trinity of experience
and it is through intimacy on earth that
you test your powers."*

Intimacy with self, with others, and through groups is the ability to allow for a trusting within your heart, an opening within your psyche, and a vulnerability within your soul.

Intimacy is a need that you share with the world – a deep need that cannot be fulfilled by touching, feeling, and joining. These feelings will not satisfy your deep need for true intimacy, which springs from your connection with the Source. Before time as you know it you were filled with the value that came from that connection.

Fear was first experienced upon this plane in the form of a thought. The thought was to close off, to turn away from, to pretend that intimacy was not essential – you believed that God had abandoned you.

These are old feelings that come from a time when you believed you could be rejected, judged, hurt. You are no longer a child, you need fear nothing. As a god, however, you seek to experience everything. Each of you reading these words feels the need to share your experiences with others through the connection of sharing.

The groups you will form, be it only self and another, come to-gether in order to express and experience vulnerability, trusting, and to know that there is nothing to fear outside of self. It is with this final lesson that Transformation will be experienced. For when you have recognized the fact that you are invulnerable, you will be restored to the inheritance that has waited for you these many thousands of years.

Your birthright is your assurance that you cannot be harmed by other and that you are harmless to all, that you fear nothing and have not the capacity to make another living thing fearful. You suffer only by your own hand, your own thoughts, and your own deeds.

You need no longer control nor manipulate the world outside of self through your threats, through your attacks, through your pre-tense of powerlessness. Instead it is a privilege to know who you are, to experience self as a complete, whole, abundant being who has everything and fears nothing. Through this knowledge may you gain the experience and correct use of your divine power, knowing it flows from Source to substance.

Substance is what you be, Source is what you have been, and Love is what you are becoming. This is the trinity of experience and it is through intimacy on earth that you test your powers.

You fear expansion through intimacy with others because you believe you cannot be truthful, open, honest, or forthright with another. You believe that to do so would weaken and lessen self and empower and strengthen other.

Your world is one of illusion and opposites. What the mind judges about your behaviour and finds unacceptable, it then formulates into a belief that must be projected outward onto another for the purpose of experiencing itself as correct.

But the mind has no power over truth expressed. It is incapable of altering the truth you share with God. The ego can only make you believe that to experience intimacy would be your death. Once, however, you have allowed yourself the wonder of the connection through intimacy, your experience will be one of understanding. For it is through intimacy with other that you will understand that all that dies is the ego and with it pain, separation, fear, and loneliness.

The ego would have you believe you are weak and fearful, but this is precisely why you must always confront fears. It is in the confrontation that you will realize there is no truth found in fears.

Through your willingness to disregard the ego's voice, regardless of how legitimate its message appears, you will experience a new truth and you will find again your connection with the Source. Do not listen to the voice of the ego, who would convince you that other is not as valuable as you. If you continue to deny value to other, it is you who will feel worthless.

The ego would have you believe that you are strong when you ask for no assistance. It would have you believe that you are together when you stand apart. It would have you believe you are whole when you are alone.

Risk through intimacy now that you may receive your greatest truth. Release your fears through trusting, knowing that you are trustworthy. Maintain your mask of strength through arrogance no more, for it is fragile as the clay from which your ego is made. That which stands behind the mask is invincible and wishes to join again with the Source. The gains you make now are the ego's loss. It is the ego that keeps you from your discovery of the path of intimacy.

You who are known as the whole of humanity are formed from the Source and you are one. The One has fragmented itself and through the madness of its individual egos looks outward and sees the many. It is time for this group to experience the trust the world wishes for itself. Each in this group has agreed to be the accurate reflection for another.

The group as a whole is now asked to support the one so that they may discover what they share together.

It is safe for you to share, to trust, to ask, to love, to show self. It is dangerous to pretend, to defend, to lie, to distance yourself.

Go today and be intimate within self. Lovingly witness all your characteristics and do not run from them, even if the mind speaks to you of their flaws. From this firm stance will you then be in a position to give and receive intimacy with others. Experience the new found freedom away from the pretense and postures that have been supported for lifetimes through the ego's fearful lies. From this freedom comes a release in gratitude expressed through your willingness to be intimate. Experience your own wholeness through the connection found within intimacy.

# Focus on Intimacy

Your most intimate relationship is between yourself and your Source. Your consciousness holds the connection between you both. Getting to know, trust and honor the self is the first step in extending those qualities to others.

Meditation is the practice of patience and persistence for the purpose of expanding personal and limited perception into universal and transcended consciousness. Through meditation you begin to glimpse your truest and deepest nature, one you share with the Source of all substance. Each time you still yourself and move more into a place of peace you become part of another way of knowing and being known. This is intimacy on its highest level.

Get to know the you that is larger than your current definition of self. However, you have defined yourself in the past is a limitation of the light that lives through you now. Greater awareness of self brings you out of your own shadow of fear and separation, and instead into a conscious committed connection with all creation.

For the next seven days ask yourself this question over and over with each and every breathe you take during your meditation practice. "Who am I?" The mind will quickly respond with an answer such as "mother, sister, daughter, worker", but these are relationships with others, and do not define who you are in being. As long as you receive an answer you know you have not reached deeply enough. Eventually, as you ask you will begin to know that you are literally beyond the limitation of labels, or of the roles you play in life. As you move closer toward this new definition of self, you will find more intimacy in your life.

Each evening read this affirmation so that you might remember who you truly are.

> *I am content now,*
>
> *intimate with myself.*
>
> *A Source that flows freely*
>
> *and floods toward my finite self.*
>
> *As a lake does not wish*
>
> *to be a mountain.*
>
> *So too am I at peace.*
>
> *For in the lake is mirrored the mountain*
>
> *and in me is reflected the unity of One*
>
> *and the essence of All.*
>
> *Joyously, I embrace the entirety of myself as I AM.*

# TRANSFORMATION

# Transplanting Self

*"Transformation is not radical nor revolutionary – it is subtle and gentle and it rests within your mind all the time."*

Gratefully acknowledge your arrival into Transformation. In truth you have simply transplanted yourself once again where you belong.

Tradition is a word of rigidity and stagnation, allowing no movement, no way to expand or alter experience. And so it was necessary for you to transport yourself out of Tradition and into Transition so that you might provide the movement necessary in order to reach Transformation.

Yet remember that once you have left Tradition you become responsible for redefining reality. Let it be understood that when we speak of the movement or shift that occurs during Transition it is actually effected through stillness and non-action. So it is in the same way that we now speak of Transformation, which may take place without visible signs of outer change.

Transformation is an alteration through inner resolve. Transformation changes the function but not necessarily the form of all things. Because during your Transition you allowed yourself a time for inner reflection, you may now experience Transformation.

Transformation begins as a shift within the perception of its user.

That change in perception is then translated through the design as a change in function. Transformation is a change in the nature or character of a thing without a subsequent change in structure. Transformation is not radical nor revolutionary – it is subtle and gentle and it rests within your mind all the time.

Tradition is rooted in time and space and as such has its origins upon this planet. Tradition is not known in other dimensions, for there exists no past on which to base present actions, only the continuous now. Transition is the receptive time of germination that eventually delivers itself into Transformation. Transformation is the inner joy of expansion naturally attempting to express itself outwardly.

Remember, the more simple the message, the more meaningful the lesson. See Tradition as the slow, drab, earthbound body of the caterpillar, and view Transition as the receptive patience of its cocoon as the spirit within attempts to transform and prepare for its destiny of free flight.

Though your eyes would not let you behold the vision, the essence of the butterfly is found within the worm. Like you, the butterfly shares the cycles of ascendancy mastering all the various stages. Unlike you, however, the butterfly knows from its inception its divine destiny and, holding firmly the clarity of that vision, manifests it.

Transformation is only a natural realignment of the divine purpose held within and that of its physical form without. That inner shift will often cause the outer appearance to change, but this is not always called for. In Tradition the context is changed, never its content.

True Transformation is not achieved through the outer form but rather by the shift in perception that then alters its nature or character so as to create a new direction, a new destiny. It is not the container but its contents that create the consequences found on your planet.

What gives form meaning upon this plane? It is your mind that is allowed to label, to define, to prescribe use. Yet by its very nature the mind is attached to its own security and rooted in traditional values. The mind is limited and so projects that limitation onto everything it sees.

All things upon your plane possess within them the power to heal and to teach. Within each inanimate object lives a wisdom that will divulge itself to you if you would receive it in a new way, if you would but alter your perception of how teaching might come about and by whom you might be taught. Each thing that has its origin upon this plane contains within it the essence of positive purpose placed there by the Source. There is a piece of God held within everything and everything is held within the peace of God.

This then is the true essence, the one definition which most accurately reflects the purest intentions of its creator. It is your responsibility to recognize the spirit essence and disregard the physical appearance. It is from this new perspective that miracles are created.

There is no single use for any object. Yet your mind has so limited the value of all its sees that it holds each object captive within Tradition. Indeed, there is a traditional purpose for all things and you know it well, but there is also a transitional or healing purpose for all things and a transformational or teaching purpose for all things.

You will soon see the new dawn for humankind. You have already in place the technologies necessary to realize your greatest vision, your grandest dream. Today, not the next century. Today, no one need starve, no one need die, no one need live within oppressive systems, no one need labour for another for rewards that hold no value. There need be no war, no disease, no greed, jealousy, or envy; all may receive equally the bounty that abounds in an Unbound world.

Do these words stir hope or disbelief within you? Do you wish this could be possible, only to know that it is not? Your consciousness is the vehicle that will transport your world into Transformation, right now. You have everything; what you lack is the courage to live it creatively. Why would anyone wish to relive over and over the nightmare of poverty, prejudice, war, disease, and death? The mind, beloved, projects its own version of insanity and the world reflects it back to you for the purpose of possible revision.

Your political and economic systems are changing to reflect the new view their users see for them. Each of you has had your insight restored through the willingness to receive these messages. These teachings help you to remember where you must look in order to witness the part you have agreed to play in the transformation of the world.

There are four principles that, when accepted by the many, shall create a new reality for all. These principles are the belief in reincarnation and eternal life, that you and God are unified in spirit and so connected through the body, that there is no limitation or scarcity in the world, that the purpose of life is to express through joy and experience pleasure.

The raised vibration produced through the living of these principles shall cause a shift to be felt within the very foundation of Tradition. Up through the cracks will seep the transfusion of new energy that will create a different destiny.

*Many and Varied Lifetimes:* Recognize that there is no death, only the continuous unfolding of life and there will be no reason for the fearful belief in hell, or the hopeful one of a heaven in a hereafter. Inherent within this belief called reincarnation shall be the acceptance of the correctness found in all circumstances in which you are involved.

No blame falls on another, and neither may you see your position as powerless. Instead you realize that you cause and create it all in order to learn – taking its lesson and moving on. Who would you envy or condemn if you knew that you had played every role – Pope and pauper, black and white, assassin and aristocrat?

*God Lies Within:* When you recognize that you are God you awaken within yourself all the divine attributes you have given to God. You need not suffer, nor cause any living thing to suffer. You are free to express your own unlimitedness. If God were within, what religion would you need, what denomination would you support? What monuments would your contributions help build, if you knew that your body houses the divine spirit and your heart is its altar?

*Bounty and Abundance:* From the belief that you are a god, you would be granted a faith in existence's ability to provide. You would realize your powers of creativity and manifestation and never again experience lack. There would be no shortage of time, of money, of power, of employment. No one could have what you wanted, for you are the source of all that you need.

*The Joyful Expression of Life:* The basic purpose of life is to provide experience for your spirit through feelings that flow from the choices you may make on this plane. When you are done with this process, as each of you has been for lifetimes, it is then your purpose to express it courageously, outwardly, through joyousness.

You are on an adventure of the soul. There is nothing to fear, for you cannot be harmed nor can you harm, you have already received forgiveness for acts you are incapable of committing, and you are the eternal vessel through whom the divine has chosen to manifest. Failure in this divine experiment is impossible, for you

153

need only open, embrace, expand, and fill yourself with more life in order to succeed, and this is your very nature.

Transformation is a stage of the Cycle of Ascendancy created for the purpose of displaying dreams. Transformation is instantaneous – it is available to you for it exists in the present moment. You need only alter your attitude in order to be transformed. The more present you are in the moment, the more you aid the world in its transformation. Examine your perceptions, the reflections of your beliefs, before you attempt to change anything in the outside world as you know it.

Transformation may only become a reality when you believe that dreams really can come true. Know this: every thought you think becomes reality, every dream you dream comes true, every wish you wish is fulfilled, every hope you hold happens, every image you imagine is materialized. Your experience this lifetime and the next and the next will be the sum total of what you think, dream, wish, imagine, and hope.

These simple sentences express the prayers of the world. Choose again – you are always free to do so. Through your willingness to be courageous and choose a different direction, a new purpose, a clearer focus you are then free to experience a new future.

Each of you is a transformer. You hold within you the energy, the clarity, the compassion, and the insight necessary to restore the vision of sanity to the world. Deny yourself nothing you truly want, so that you might give the world what it deserves. Transcend the mundane and traditional view the world holds of itself through the power of your decision to do so; your resolve makes all things accessible, possible.

Peace is the greatest hope held upon your plane at this time. Peace is not a dream but a promise from the Divine and given to you at creation. Yet you have believed another who says that peace is a dream you do not deserve. Peace is no dream, it is a personal guarantee from the Creator.

Peace cannot be negotiated nor won. It cannot be negotiated for you may never bargain or deal for it, nor may it be won for you could never lose it. If you did not believe that another could give peace to you, you would never have allowed it to be taken from you. Instead know that peace is your heritage, your birthright.

You create peace through the living of your vision and you pass peace on through providing another with the possibility of living theirs. If you refuse to live your dream you halt the process for peace. You are the eternal channel through which peace flows. You are the essential link in the chain of peace.

We ask that you do only one thing in the coming weeks in order to produce Transformation in your lives – close your eyes when you see only Tradition. Close the physical eyes when you are confronted with anything that does not enhance the vision you hold within. Close the physical eyes and in that instant remind yourself that what you see is not the truth, only the last vestiges of an illusion fading away.

Power is with the One. The effective self shall transform the world. Everything is now in place; we wait for you to turn around and share what you have with others. The power of the One – from the singleness of your purpose, the clarity of your intention, the veracity of your vision – shall create in the many a realization that peace is already present.

Each of you has believed that a dream could be destroyed. You have all experienced the consequences of Atlantis and have now returned to fulfill your Karmic responsibility to the restoration of peace. It is time to remember the reason for which you have returned.

Through the use of the pyramidal structure you created awesome monuments that were left behind as gifts to remind the earth of what was possible. It is now time to restore the mystical purpose of the pyramid. It is time to transform the pyramid into a living principle of power, to elevate it to its intended purpose.

In Atlantis you believed that you were powerless, that the dream could die. The dream can never die, as long as the dreamer lives. You are the dreamkeepers who have returned to resume their dreaming. Yet this time the dreamers will awaken and realize the dream has already come true.

You believe that the ego, displaying as an individual, has power over the many. This is the traditional view the world has adopted through the hierarchical use of the pyramid.

Within this structure there is only room for one leader while all else must mindlessly follow. We ask that you transform this traditional concept of the pyramid and so allow its powerful forces to aid you. You are the powerful conduit through which peace passes and the pyramid shall make it possible.

See instead the One sharing the light within themselves so that the many might be ignited by that passion from the flame of desire. See that from the light produced by the One, the many might find within themselves a vision which was before overshadowed in darkness. See the One, not as savior, but as sharing a sense of self. See the One embracing and holding the many through the promise of prosperity and peace for all. The One may not keep for itself what is not reflected back to it by the many. The many joined together in wholeness are without lack.

Transformation begins with the One, who being so complete reflects that wholeness within self to another who is instantly healed, who being so complete reflects that wholeness within self to another who is healed, who being so complete reflects that wholeness within self to another who is healed, and on without end to another and another. The mystical body of Christ is found in the structure of the pyramid, and you are its beginning.

Before you have been as worms groveling in the dust of Tradition, unwilling to recognize the truth of what lies dormant within, waiting to arise. The caterpillar would not know how to proceed if it were not able to see a part of itself within the vision expressed by another butterfly.

The butterfly that is free stands as the perfect reflection for the worm of what "might be" and through this insight the worm is awakened to its own inner vision and beauty. Each time you refuse to live your vision you deny the reflective light to one who cannot as yet see it in themselves. Millions are denied their dream because they cannot see clearly without the light you hold within.

Thy light is come and the glory of God is risen within you. Arise, sun/Son of God, and go forth without fear. You cannot fail in your mission, for those who are with you are more than those who are against you. When you are with yourself, none may stand apart. The light of dawn is breaking and with it shall come a New Age. You are the way, the truth, and the light.

# Focus on Transformation

Oftentimes what is regarded as truth is in fact only a belief. Perception and not reality is what most of us deal with. Your perceptions and beliefs may be altered in order to create a new experience. If you are to stay in Transformation you must always be challenging yourself in new and expanded ways.

List the areas in your life that cause you difficulty such as finances, relationships, health, labour. Then write down all your beliefs about them – everything that you were told was true, everything that has been your experience as true, everything you believe to be true.

When you have finished, look at the list and realize that these beliefs shape your experience and create your reality. The way you can prove this to yourself is to see that if your beliefs were really true then everyone in the world would have the same experience. Clearly they don't. Some people hold beliefs that result in prosperity, others are destitute. While it is easy for some to create loving relationships, others hold beliefs that say there is scarcity. Some people are always healthy, others are constantly ill.

Do not allow your mind to convince you that it is random external causes that create these differences. It is the internally held beliefs. You need only change your beliefs in order to change your experience.

Now choose one area on the list in which you would like to create a new experience for yourself. Look at your beliefs and begin to write an affirmation beside each one. Refute your own beliefs. Have a real argument with yourself. Take a positive position that might lead you in the direction you say you want to go.

For instance, perhaps it is your experience that you are accident prone; then look to the belief that you are clumsy. When you have identified the belief that locks the behaviour into place, then argue with yourself against it. Become conscious of all the times you haven't injured yourself rather than the few times you have and affirm those. Realize that you have selectively chosen to see reality and that it is possible to change it by affirming a new truth.

Know that you are either confirming all your old patterns or you are affirming new ones. Confirmation holds you in Tradition – affirmation delivers you into Transformation.

Miracles are made with the mind.

# Imagination and Creativity

*"Imagination is that calm space*
*within your being that receives images*
*transmitted from a higher dimension of*
*self, guidance towards Transformation."*

These words are only as real as you can imagine. In order for you to recognize them you must trust that remembrance that lives as an image reflected in the third eye called imagination. It is through your imagination that you shall know reality, as you fearlessly look for the truth that can be found beyond physical appearance.

Each person must seek their own release from the tradition found in the mind. Each must find within self a space from which Transformation may emerge. This then shall be the process necessary to produce evolvement within the individual. Planetary evolution, however, is dependent upon the willingness of those individuals to lend themselves as open channels for higher energy. That higher energy shall forever be known as creativity.

Transformation is fashioned from the creative mind of one who has traveled within the Cycle of Ascendancy and emerged triumphant. Transformation is found as a vibratory level of awareness that extends out of the creative mind and influences all things that surround it on a physical level.

Tradition exists primarily through your sensory perception. Transition asks that you still those senses, that you quiet the mind so that you might experience what is beyond the activity of the senses. Transformation is then created from the space discovered during Transition and then enlarged so as to envelop your entire outer life. Transformation is constantly creative, never automatic in its response.

Imagination is that calm space within your being that receives images transmitted from a higher dimension of self, guidance towards Transformation. While in this heightened state of awareness called imagination, solutions are found to all your problems. Problems exist as earthbound teachers that attempt to lead you to this place called imagination through which you might then experience a transformation of your difficulties.

You create difficulties, problems, questions so that you might transcend the mundane and travel into the mystical. These self-manifested obstacles are your guides upon this journey into your own creative process. This creative process will eventually lead you toward your destiny. For each time you allow your imagination to free itself and venture out into the higher realms in order to retrieve the answers and then return, you are charting your own course homeward.

See your difficulties for what they really are – opportunities to project your consciousness into the higher regions. Yet most of you when besieged by difficulties become overwhelmed and venture only as far as your closest addictions. At times of stress you search for some substance that will transform your experience into a "high." It is not oblivion you seek, although the mind repeatedly leads you down that path, but rather the "high" of expanded awareness that is possible when you move out of your mind and into the realm of the inspired.

All things come to those who willingly open themselves in order to receive. In order to become open and receptive you must be willing to trust that indeed there is something of significance ready to be delivered. Do not discourage its delivery through your doubt over your own value. Instead simply decide to trust. Trust is found in the expanding heart that always hopes. Doubt is always found in a desperate mind. The mind is desperate to deny you your deliverance. Please use your head for the purpose for which it was intended.

Transform your use of the mind, the body, the emotions, and the spirit. The mind was given to you as a magnificent tool for identifying and defining difficulties, for analyzing and sorting sensory perceptions, and most importantly as a tool for manifesting divine directives.

The mind cannot give you peace, cannot see your vision, and is incapable of creating real solutions. You have simply asked the mind to give you what it does not have. In constantly deferring to your mind during times of crisis you have created a tyrant whose sole goal is to continue its reign.

It is your job in Transformation to alter, to vary, and to change the function given to the mind from one of tyrant to one of technical advisor. No longer run to your mind for solace, for comfort, for consolation. Simply change your mind and by so doing you shall be in possession of a miracle instantly.

The mind is a superb recorder of past deeds. These deeds are analyzed, evaluated, and always found lacking. The mind is judgmental and as such always perceives you as guilty. The mind then willingly shares this guilt by projecting it onto all it surveys. The mind believes in guilt by association. You are not your mind.

Your deliverance through the mind is impossible for it does not believe you are deserving. The heart holds the vaster view of your eternal perfection and so is free to show you an accurate reflection.

The cloud of doubt is always found in the mind but is soon passed on to the spirit to infect it with hopelessness. Hope of the heart is overshadowed by the darkness of doubt in the mind. The mind has convinced you that doubt is only discernment and that without its capacity to doubt you would be left adrift, defenseless in a hostile world bent on your destruction.

But doubt is what keeps you from experiencing your own divine destiny. You hear the call a thousand times a day through the imagination, intuition, and inspiration, and you deny it. So we ask that during Transformation you doubt nothing that comes from within.

Doubt nothing seen within your imagination, doubt nothing felt within the inspiration of your own heart, doubt nothing heard within the intuition of your own knowingness, doubt nothing that God sends to you through the shared connection of creativity.

If you must doubt, then doubt all those things that are seen, heard, felt, sent to you from the outer world. And when you have doubted those things, then kindly use the mind and doubt your own doubtfulness. Your difficulties may only be overcome through your trusting that there is a solution accessible to you.

Transformation is a dimension of altered awareness that is accessible to all through the trusting of their own imaginative process. All have the ability; none are denied.

No one has more capacity than another to touch their own divinity. It is simply a willingness to allow the creative energy of the One Source to be channeled openly and uniquely into the consciousness expressing individually.

Sit still and know that you are a part of God. You will know this through the communication called imagination – the process of creativity and inspiration. Meditation opens the door to your higher centers. Close your eyes, shut your mouth, disengage from the world of form, and open yourself instead to creative spirit.

Creative energy is the highest energy form you may receive while in physical form upon this plane. Through the creative energy as expressed through the actions of those in body, this planet will be transformed. Creative energy heals, expands, transmutes, and enlightens. As the recipient of creative energy it is your responsibility to acknowledge your receipt through action. It is your shared means of connection with God, and the way you channel it is unique and essential to the transformation of the world.

Creativity takes courage and commitment. Creative energy once channeled into Tradition transforms it. The very survival of the earth is now in jeopardy. As her guardian you have been entrusted with the retrieval of a vision, uniquely yours, that must then be translated from inner fantasy to outer form.

Through thousands of years that you call your history you have destroyed the dreamers and denied their dreams of love, peace, beauty, and joy. These things are only seen as dreams upon a planet that believes instead in the reality of its experience of anger, rage, hatred, greed, envy, fear, and pain. Remember that what is real lies within, and that what is held with conviction must manifest without.

For too long the leaders of this planet have allowed their lower senses to serve as the only means of identifying reality. They look to the experiences of the past in order to form their belief in the future. In so doing they really recreate their fathers' fears.

Instead we ask that you close your eyes for a moment on the illusions of the world. Listen to your intuition, see with your imagination, feel through your inspiration. Together they will combine to create the substance from which dreams are fashioned. Then, when you have received your dream, your vision, open your eyes and with the assistance of the focused mind translate it with courage and determination outward toward the waiting world.

What is real is eternal. What is eternal is the dreamer and the dream. In order for your dream to come true, you must now arise and awaken to your imagination and creativity.

You are responsible for the salvation of the world through the courageous living of your dream. It is through your creativity that sanity will be restored here on earth.

Do not doubt your essential part in this drama. Only consider for a moment what keeps you from your own destiny. What is more precious than awaking within yourself to your own mission? What fears of failure keep you from proceeding? What do you believe you will be asked to sacrifice – money, prestige, possessions, security, approval?

Look seriously at the bargain you have cast in your life for these items. Attached to each of these supposed treasures is the price of pain, guilt, worry, anger, and the fear of loss. You have already lost, beloved, when you refuse yourself the right to play.

To live creatively means to overcome obstacles, to literally come over the objections presented by the fearful mind and to rely solely upon inner direction. Creativity asks you to expand yourself beyond your own momentary experience so that ultimately it may be transformed. This you may do, when you call upon the guidance that is available to you in the higher realms of the creative process.

Look again at the moment in which you find yourself and if it does not appear to you to be in keeping with your deepest desires for health, happiness, and wholeness, then go back to the source and create it again. As long as you be in body, you are always free to change your mind, to choose a new direction, and create a new reality.

It is your spirit that should select the vision to be viewed, not your mind. The mind is the projector, and the universe is your screen. You may always see the results you create in the world. It is then only a simple procedure of proper alignment within your being that promotes peace and provides balance in your life.

However, in the version of the world you know, the mind commands control producing a nightmare from its own paranoid fears. Because you have free will to choose, your spirit is rendered helpless and the earth is forced to experience this horror.

The program you see in the outer world was designed by the mind. If the program is less than hoped for, do not curse and complain to the screen on which it is being projected or to the manufacturer. Instead go to your mind, the source of your difficulty, disconnect the circuitry, and choose again.

You are given two ways to do this. You may create a new future through your disengaging of your creative energy flow within the particular situation – simply walk away. Or you may remain within the situation and choose to transform its very character through your creative resources – forgiveness. Regardless of your choice, your first obligation is to awaken self sufficiently so as to recognize that all change is effected through divine intervention called creativity.

In order to activate your creative process you must first perceive that the difficult situation is merely an effect caused by the limited thinking of the mind and not, as some feel, the punishment of God or randomness of the universe. When you have changed your mind in this regard, you have freed your imagination to expand beyond the seen into the unseen.

Each new day you are offered an opportunity to arise and to choose a new future. Daybreak casts a totally new light on past problems. For some on your planet, sleep is the only state in which reception is possible. We ask that you bring more consciousness to your awakened states of creativity.

Many are the number of those who are unconscious of their jobs as tributaries of incoming creative energy upon your planet. Those who exhibit this lifetime as female and engaged in relationship have a responsibility to channel shared creative visions.

There is a specified time during their cycle that is clocked and counted by the moon, when they are most receptive to this creative clarity. They are then to transmit, through psychic resolve, the messages to their male counterpart who is to manifest them in form. The earth is experiencing much chaos in relationships due to the reluctance of the female who is to receive and the resistance of the male who is then to respond.

Also lost are the children. Your children, look at how they hurry to "grow up." Growing up in your world is synonymous with growing out of the gentle creative inner flow and instead into the turbulent tides of popular opinion found in the outer world. But before they grow up, before their instincts are repressed, they are free to create their entire experience out of the boundless fantasy of another dimension. Fantasy is the acting out that breathes God's love into formless dreams.

Few on your planet believe in fantasy or fairies, in magic or mysticism, in visions, in spirits, in legend and lore, in rituals and ceremonies; few believe in the power of the goddess or the crystal. The women and children who in the past have brought to this plane with them the belief in the unseen magic of the mystical have forgotten why they have come. It is time to bring into balance the real with the unreal.

What is held within your healing heart is truth. Reality is only a fantasy forming itself into fact through the desire of the dreamer to experience it.

There is a higher level of awareness through which you may transform this plane of physical form. Access to this higher dimension is achieved through the imagination. You recreate your existing world from the fantasy of the unseen, from the beauty of the imaginative.

You have dominion over all things through the creative process. Your physical world is only a world within a world from which is drawn the patterns, the shapes, the designs that are then brought

167

back to this world and assembled into your own form of reality. The entirety of your material world, no matter how substantial it may appear to the physical eyes, is in reality only an extension of an idea created out of the unseen dimensions.

Just as your consciousness was created through the desire of the Divine to express an idea of love to itself, so all of your creations are divine ideas expressing through your desire to experience them in time and space. Physical reality is only a temporary means of transplanting from the higher vibrations to this lowered one.

The reason that physical matter is not permanent on this plane is that it does not have its origins here. What you experience as entropy is in reality only a natural process of reclamation. It is returning to its higher vibratory dimension, fading from this one. You see, your world is in transformation constantly. Yet there is nothing that needs change but your direction, your focus, your alignment, your choice – nothing need change, beloved, but the perceptions found in your mind.

You are the creative principle expressed by a loving God. During creation there was placed within your soul a vision. It is your only mission this lifetime to go within and retrieve it. You are on a glorious quest to realms where your imagination shall reign supreme, but it is through your heart that you will be shown the way.

# Focus on Creativity

Everything in the physical world was first an idea, a vision in imagination. Whatever you wish to create in your life must first be imagined vividly. It is known that creativity is a function of the right brain responsible for intuition, inspiration, artistic ability, and imagination.

In order to become more creative you need only access that part of yourself that houses creativity. Most of the traditional ways of learning do not facilitate the creative process. You cannot list, analyze, define, or diagram your way to creativity. Instead it must be subtly coaxed through processes that are quite different from the way you are used to learning.

To be more creative you need to believe that you are creative. It is a self fulfilling prophecy. Creative people are daydreamers who don't believe that fantasies are a waste of time. Use your imagination, flights of fantasy, make up fairy tales, anything whimsical and fun. Visualization and guided imagery are powerful techniques that assist your creative imagination:

The creative mind is like a muscle that has atrophied. Very few things in our culture support creativity. More often conformity and competition are rewarded. In order to rebuild the natural ability you had as a creative child you need to use your imagination in a conscious and focused way.

Visualizations give you an opportunity to see it clearly in your head so that you might feel it with desire in your being and project it out into the world as your physical experience.

# Acceptance, Alignment, and Attunement

*"Accept, align, and attune. When
you have mastered these three simple
processes, the light you call enlightenment
will shine within your being."*

Greetings, beloved who travels the path of Transformation.

Transformation occurs through an alteration in attitude and perception. This change comes when you shift your focus from outer knowledge to inner knowing. Regard your imagination as the window to view this inner world.

Creativity is the energy that transforms the traditional into the transcended, the mundane into the mystical. The hope of your planet rests within the creative minds of its inhabitants. No longer hold out hope that another might provide it for you. Peace is your purpose, receiving it your responsibility.

Creativity is the greatest resource available upon your planet. What your world perceives as valuable is often in fact worthless. You believe that value is determined by scarcity – the less available the more valuable. This is insanity posing as prosperity. Those things that hold real value, beloved, are unlimited and accessible to all.

Creativity can never be qualified nor controlled. It is an endless source to all whose hearts are willing to receive. When each beloved is in touch with their own intuitive process, judgment, jealousy, greed, and theft will serve no purpose for all will create from their purest intentions and each according to their own needs.

There is fast approaching a time upon this planet when only those creative souls who are willing to open their hearts and minds in order to receive shall be allowed to remain – a time when the meek shall truly inherit the earth. Those who continue to disregard the integrity of their spirit shall cause to create an assault upon their body and remove themselves from this dimension.

Make yourself meek through your receptivity. Still the senses, subdue the emotions, silence the mind, so that you might once again support the spirit. Through your intuition you shall reclaim your connection with the Creator.

Intuition will connect you with your divine memory and so grant you the four essential elements of Transformation upon this planet – creativity, compassion, commitment, and courage. This energy flows: Creator, creative, creation to consciousness. This is how you have come to be formed, the creative force continuously attempting to know itself.

Through the process of imagination you bring into your being a vibrational quality that identifies you with the New Age of Transformation. Imagination and creativity shall create a current of love that floods your being with light. It is from this light that extraordinary events will be attracted.

Creativity is found only in the moment and transforms the future into the present perfect. You will no longer be allowed to postpone your own happiness and so deny the world your joy. Instead redirect your energy to this moment and know that from it will you receive everything you will need later on.

Creativity is the elevated feeling, the connection, the love for which you all search. Because you have asked, there has been and will continue to be an infusion of intense energy into your planet.

This energy is felt within your being as a high frequency, a strong resonance, a sharp pitch or tone. The energy itself is neutral, beloved, and so you are free to create from it any reality you wish.

The vibration is from the Source and as such speaks directly to the spirit asking that you become still and surrendered. Yet many deny the signals and disregard their spirit, refusing to surrender their egos. Instead, they move away from spirit and out toward substance.

Since they search for Source through substance their satisfaction is impossible and they become abused. The world insists that the individual abuses the substance, when clearly the intention is to be abused. Regardless, your plane will continue to produce addicts in epidemic proportion until those who abuse themselves realize they already have what they search for.

The earth plane is desperate for this elevated energy. You must help disseminate it. Distribution of this essential energy is achieved through your meditation, your dreams, your prayers, your imagination, your intuition, your creativity. Your intentions serve as magnets moving the energy around. Through the use of small groups you are all becoming visionary channels for society as well as self.

How might one invite and so channel more of this powerful force into their lives? Simply accept, align, and attune. These are the raw materials that shall construct a new reality.

It is so simple, but the mind chooses to see the simple as obscure. Nothing of meaning is found in the meandering of the mind. Cease from running to the mind for the answers to questions it makes up to drive you mad.

Instead accept, align, and attune. Accept your own divinity. Align your four essential bodies. Attune yourself to your own inner knowingness.

Accept your real identity, and not the pathetic picture painted by the mind from a palette colored by projection. The mind can give you no accurate portrait of who you are for it is tinged by its own belief in separation, fear, guilt, sacrifice, and pain. The mind will always portray you as limited. Accept instead the truth the heart holds. Accept the help that surrounds you constantly. Accept yourself and the promise of Transformation you have come to deliver.

Acceptance places your entire being within the healing vibration of receptivity. It creates a current within you of communion. Acceptance allows you to surrender to your own nurturing spirit. Through the quality of acceptance you are made meek. Acceptance unifies all things in love.

Align your four essential bodies – physical, mental, emotional, and spiritual. Each of these presents you with its own unique gift called sensation. Yet when each is aligned they shall together give you the greatest gift of all – balance. When you experience balance in your life you will remember the reason for your coming which was placed within your soul prior to your incarnation. Your four essential bodies shall quite literally hold the combination necessary to unlock the secret found in your soul. Alignment is achieved through acceptance of the purpose of each of the bodies.

Attune your conscious mind inward so that it might remember the celebration of the spirit and the satisfaction found in the soul. Silence the salacious mind and listen instead to the purity in the heart that speaks of peace and wholeness. Attune yourself to the will of God.

Accept, align, and attune. When you have mastered these three simple processes, the light you call "enlightenment" will shine within your being. This light within signifies a love for the Source as manifested through the self. Mastery is found in acceptance, alignment, and attunement, and it is available to all.

In the past you have believed your body to be a burden; you have allowed your mind to torment you and your emotions to attack you. You have been out of alignment with the greatest tools given to you for your own transformation. Accept yourself and the responsibility for the quest you have undertaken. Align your body, mind, emotion, and spirit, acknowledging them to be the selfless servers waiting to transport you toward your destination. Attune and adjust your focus so that you might receive the divine wisdom that will transform your experience to heaven on earth.

*The Physical Body:* Align your body and experience the beauty of its creation, a beauty beyond words. Glorious are the workings of the body human. The body shall be called a joy by all those who have ever been held within her form for even one moment and through that experience shall they have gained a new perspective and wisdom.

The harmony found within the body shall be an example to those who listen to her unique song and know it to be from God. Never again from any of the other planes will you be given a gift of greater magnitude. Never again in all the galaxies to which you shall travel will you find a greater guide. In all the journeys yet to come will you never be better and more humbly served than by this, your body.

The body is the transporter of the soul, the vehicle of the psyche, the navigator of your journey – a great server who receives little for the services rendered. The body desires only one thing: to partake of her own destiny. The destiny of the body is unrestricted movement. To move openly, freely, expansively. To express herself in health and through the physical achievements for which she was uniquely created.

The body is a miracle that shall act as your interpreter in this land where the native language is one of feelings and sensations. In order for your body to function it must be given a free rein of movement, what you call exercise.

Through movement the body is charged with positive energy. Movement and action create a connection with the moment. When you move you are fully present within the body and capable of receiving divine creative energy in the moment. The Source is always generating and sending infinite amounts of this energy which you may use to construct anything you wish.

It is your responsibility to clear a channel in order to receive accurate communication. For the messages that you receive in moments of movement are ones of power and glory to both your body and soul.

The physical body's perfection shall be seen through her ability to move and breathe and this will then be reflected in her well-being and radiant health. Move the body regularly; the more you move the more she will love to move. The body is childlike in her joyful need to express.

Move the body vigorously so that the lungs are expanded to capacity for a minimum of twenty minutes. When you draw in breath you are receiving inspiration directly from the divine. After exercising, become conscious of the body's heightened sensitivity; you have restored her very nature.

When you do not move the body with only the purpose of movement for the body in mind, you break down the essence of her system. When you resist moving the body, you halt the movement in other areas of your life. You cannot love God nor your brothers and sisters more than you love your body. You cannot abandon your body and expect to find God. You cannot abuse your body and then offer to do service for others. Move your body until she is fully satiated, then move into your mental body.

*The Mental Body:* Align your mind and you will have a powerful tool for manifestation and sense perception. It carries out with superb effectiveness the details of your day-to-day functions. It analyzes, directs, formulates, organizes, and reasons. The mind seeks to understand, to maintain, to protect your sense of self.

The mind, however, is not capable of initiating truth, but only of analyzing information given through the sense perceptions. The mind shall forever see separation, disease, death, and destruction. From this evidence it then postulates beliefs that are projected outward onto the world so that it might affirm its perceptions.

The mind has for too long been allowed to direct the destiny of your entire being. This the mind cannot do. For too long, limited beliefs prescribed by the mind have been allowed to be projected onto a defenseless body. The body is left then with no alternative but to out picture these reoccurring thoughts upon its flesh. The body is always the obedient servant of the mind.

For proper alignment within the mental body you must exercise it. Give it directions and information so that it may understand more fully. Once given that understanding it shall execute with authority and precision the activities of your daily life. Do not, however, allow the mind to decide your destiny, for this is not its purpose.

Align the mind with its true purpose. This you may do through meditation, prayer, and contemplation. Begin to silence the inane chattering of the mind. Twice a day, allow the mind to become clear and still through meditation. In this way it will become more open to the creative energy available.

When you disengage your mind you promote peace and harmony in the world. Do this for a minimum of twenty minutes twice a day.

*The Emotional Body:* When the mind is still and calm it will then be possible to align the emotional body. Senses and feelings are the language of your planet. Every thought in the mind is attached to a feeling or sensation. Even your soul is the recorder of your emotions on your journey called life. All memory is stored as emotion. The true nature of the emotions is to assist you on this plane with your imaginative process.

The emotions are not given to you so that you might experience suffering. You have misaligned your emotional power and are now addicted to a highly emotional view of yourself. You allow external occurrences to dictate which emotional response you will experience. Who is in control of your emotions?

The emotions are provided to help you identify what is valid for you. You need only ask within your being what is felt rather than what is thought as perfection for you, and you will be given an accurate accounting from your internal emotional charge.

The emotions are responsible for generating the power behind the imaginary process that produces materialization upon your plane. So it is ultimately through your emotions and their intense desire that you call forth from the ethers all the form that you experience on earth.

Laughter aligns the emotions with a higher vibration. Laughter is the elixir of life. It is your divine essence bubbling upward in the form of sound so that it might register upon the ears and stir the soul. Laughter is light made audible.

Laugh, for seriousness is often a mask for ignorance. Those who know the truth of this plane laugh loudly. Laugh regardless of whether or not you feel like laughing. Look for the humor in all things. Humor is a great gift and it surrounds you constantly.

*The Spiritual Body:* Align your spirit for you are spirit; your essence is drawn directly from God. Yet have you chosen to quicken that spirit into the positive contraction called embodiment. You are spirit made manifest. The nature of your soul is to experience.

Your spirit holds within its essence truth. The spirit must be allowed both its freedom and its wisdom. The soul must never be forced to exact its experiences at the expense of the body. Instead, the spirit should function as the overseer of the other three bodies upon this journey of life.

The spiritual body is your first essence from which all else is created. It is from your spiritual body that you are in direct communion with the other dimensions. The spirit is the guardian of your true mission here and left to its own devices will accurately navigate you to that destination. Your spirit must be aided, however, by the other three bodies if it is to maneuver effectively in this world of form.

You must begin to sense the enormity of the soul from which you have created the other three bodies. The soul extends itself through many planes of existence all at once, and simultaneously does it focus with precision upon the plane of earth in the form of matter.

Begin to align the spirit with its destiny through the use of forgiveness. Forgiveness aligns the soul with the vibration of the Christ who brought forgiveness to this plane.

Forgiveness is a tool with which you may continue your excavation inward toward the light. Within your impeccable being are unforgiven wounds hiding the truth of who you are. Express your wish now that you be healed in both spirit and body.

The mind withholds peace from the spirit by insisting that you are justified in your grievances, that you have been betrayed. You have indeed suffered, yet always by your own hand. Suffer no longer, free yourself through your willingness to forgive another as well as yourself.

Align the physical body through exercise, feed her properly, and allow her to breathe fully and completely. Align the mental body through meditation and dreaming. Align the emotional body through laughter and positive passion. Finally, align the spiritual body through forgiveness and service.

There was a time when you went from spirit to mass, from force to form with little more than a thought. You controlled your own consciousness, the places it traveled, the things it experienced, and the ways it expressed.

Then you became sedated through each of your embodiments. You have now lowered your vibration and forgotten the truth of who you be. Through these tools of Transformation you shall be granted the alignment necessary to restore your memory once again and reawaken your consciousness.

You are all those qualities you reserve for God. This is the truth about you, this is the truth that God identifies as you. No longer deny the Source the ability to communicate with you by your refusal to listen. You are whole, healed, and becoming Unbound. Let your thoughts, words, and deeds reflect this truth.

# Focus on Acceptance, Alignment, and Attunement

The entire universe is a symphony in balance. Within your being too is the deep part of you constantly attempting to balance itself. The formula for balance is Acceptance + Alignment + Attunement = Balance.

Resistance is the opposite of balance. When you resist, you block your own creative energies. In any situation it is essential to accept, align, and attune each of your four bodies, giving to each what is most important.

*Physical:* Provide movement and proper nutrition for the physical body. Do something out of love and concern for the physical part of yourself every day. Take a walk, exercise vigorously, ride a bicycle, have a manicure. Do something to honor your body.

*Mental:* Provide affirmations and positive thought forms for the mental body. The mind functions as a processing mechanism and it needs data in order to formulate beliefs and judgments. It doesn't care, however, what it processes, so it is up to you to feed your mind positive, uplifting, supportive information so that it might form the same type of beliefs. Write a positive statement that you would like to implement in your life. Write it 10 times in the morning and 10 times at night for 21 days and watch the view you hold of your world absolutely transform.

*Emotional:* The emotional body needs to freely express its feelings without judgment or guilt. Because we have been suspicious of our emotions, fearful that they may get out of hand and we would lose control and look foolish, we have repressed even normal emotions.

Repressed emotions get stuck in the physical body as blocks and can cause dysfunction. To unblock emotions all you have to do is tell the truth. If you begin to tell the whole truth in your life, the emotions will automatically be expressed. Do not dwell on difficulty, discomfort, or despair; just tell the truth, allow yourself to feel it, and then move on. Once emotions surface they move very quickly. Look at how fast children react, from crying to laughing in a moment.

*Spiritual:* The spiritual body depends on your channeling direct communication from the divine source within you.

The spiritual part of you loves to be rather than do. The greatest gift to spirit is giving of self.

# Passion

"*You die so soon because you are afraid to live fully. All death on your planet is a form of suicide. You would never have to die if you chose to live your life with passion.*"

Passion is a most misguided issue. Traditionally passion is equated with lust. Passion is the transforming fire contained within the heart of God. It was the Divine's desire to express passionately that caused creation to come into being.

Passion was created as intensified desire, a vibration that might express all types of feelings, physical as well as emotional. It is in that moment when you are engaged in the heightened awareness of passion that all your energy centers are open and you feel the greatest connection with the createdness.

The vibratory level contained within this life force that pulses through you becomes so strong it literally makes erect different parts of the body. We speak not only of the sexual organs, but also of the hairs, tongue, hearing; organs normally limp and flaccid become more compact and function at an accelerated level.

This transforming arousal is not confined to excitation of the loins, but occurs through anger, joy, acceptance, love, and happiness. Yet most only experience passion when involved in reproductive responses. Expansion is the purpose of living, and that power and glory you have come to know during the act of arousal should be a part of your moment-to-moment experience.

Because you are fearful of change, your lives are boring and your energy lethargic. You settle for less than you want and then complain of what you have. You have the right to live your life in an impassioned state. Your physical body is designed for this impulsive life. Your scientists are amazed at how the body's response system adjusts to sexual stimulation – how breath and heart rate increase, hearing and sight are heightened, muscularity is tightened, internal organs lessen their functions in favor of other more immediate needs – all this focused energy building to a climactic release.

The same sensation might be felt by you while in the act of even the most mundane moment of your day. There could be such a surge of excitement about all you create and experience that would build within you until it demanded a release through Transformation, a transformation that would alter the landscape of your life and transport you into a new dimension. Approach your life and embrace it with this type of passion. There was a time when each sensation felt by the body was exhilarating, each experience seemed wondrous, each movement a joy. For you, who are eternally spirit, to temporarily embody is done for the purpose of experiencing passion in physical form.

You die so soon because you do not live fully – have not lived fully for lifetime after lifetime. All death is suicide; you would never have to die if you would live your life with passion. For passion releases you into an expanded state of awareness where your connection to the Divine is found.

From this state of transcendence are all things regenerated and made new.

You think this is impossible, but what is impossible is to repress the natural instinct to live with passion in your daily life.

You are God incarnate; do you not believe that God would live a fearless, empowered, impassioned life? You are so bored by your traditional security, by your material possessions, by the seduction of your senses by illusions.

You are now insulated from your true instincts, your real feelings.

How bored you must surely be to create your climax through death and discarding the body when in fact she would live forever if you allowed her to release herself through joyful expression called passion.

Search for the meaning of life no more for it is meant to be a great joy, a mystery meant to be enjoyed not solved, an adventure for fearless gods who would choose the intensity of arousal to the numbness of death. The secret of life is contained within the desire of your spirit to experience each moment.

Search no more for the secret of everlasting life for it is found in the design and the enlightened use of the body – youthfulness is forever when life is lived with passion and zest. In this way will the body receive sufficient surges of electrical impulses from the Divine registering within and exploding with such intensity that the brain will then be charged with chemical elixirs of renewal – so more life is longed to be lived.

Transformation may be claimed today as you begin to be aroused by the sunrise, by the glorious colors in nature, by the sounds of serenity with which you are surrounded. Begin today to be excited by everything. Be lustful of the experiences you have created and claim them all boastfully.

Express yourself passionately; let everything you do be impassioned. You will sense a shift within your body that shall herald a new beginning that comes from a valued life.

When that message is received by the soul you will have touched your own divinity and be granted longevity.

Go today and live to the height of awareness for which you were created. Repress not one wish you might have to experience. Passion, when unreleased, unresolved, disregarded, or unfulfilled, contracts the body and depresses the soul. This cycle will only bring you back into Tradition expressed as repression, resentment, disease, and eventually unto death.

There is always only the same choice – life over death, passion over numbness, rejuvenation over disintegration, Transformation over Tradition!

# Focus on Passion

Sometimes we think that growing up means growing out of our passionate childlike nature. A life based on feelings of passion rather than rigid rationality can be frightening. Most of us prefer the safety and security of the predictable to the spontaneity of the passionate. To truly be receptive to the universal energy expressing itself through you is transcendence. When you are a passionate person you are responsive to the moment and responsible for every aspect of your life. Passionate people know that life is to be lived fully, deeply, purposefully, fearlessly.

Sensuality is to the spirit what sexuality is to the body. Begin to use all of your senses to bring simple pleasures back into your life. For the next seven days give yourself permission to be passionate by coming back to your senses.

1.  Taste test. Take a piece of fruit and for the next five or ten minutes do nothing but experience the sensation of taste. Imagine you have never seen, let alone ever eaten, this type of fruit before. Use each of the following activities to explore your relationship with this piece of fruit; lick, suck, drink, chew, swallow, and savor.

2.  Don't just look, see. Find a comfortable place out in nature. For the next twenty minutes let yourself see with your whole body; allow your heart to help you perceive more than just the physical beauty by which you are surrounded. Notice how your eyes can see very far away and then effortlessly refocus themselves in order to take in an image very close up. Finally, look at yourself in a mirror until you can see the strength, goodness, and beauty therein.

3.  Let yourself touch and be touched. Close your eyes and explore your environment. Let yourself experience the texture, temperature, and timbre of different items. Notice the thera-

peutic aspect of touch. With a partner use your fingers to feel their face and "see" it in a new way. Then let them touch you and experience being the recipient of touch. Are you sensitive enough to receive mental images of how things look through touch?

4. Learn to listen. With your eyes closed, place all your attention on the normal everyday sounds that surround you. Listen not only with your ears, but with your insight. Tune in to the volume and vibration that make up sounds, but also listen to silence whenever and wherever you can find it, including the silence that fills the space that is between the sounds. Notice how even silence has the ability to speak to you.

# Praise

*"Those who say they cannot make a
difference must begin to see that upon
their every word hinges the salvation of
the world. Offer praise!"*

Praise when reinforced with truth is a most powerful transforming tool for both giver and receiver – for there is no separation possible when one speaks truth.

On the earth plane scarcity appears as reality. All scarcity on the
planet originates from a lack of sincere appreciation and gratitude. When you withhold your praise you create a resistance, a
block within yourself that is then experienced by your universe
as insufficiency.

Those who receive little or no praise are greedy of keeping what
small amount of good feelings they have and so do not seek to
share themselves with others through praise. Thus the cycle of
limitation is begun. It is a traditional view of your world that
those who need praise from another are in an inferior position.
Yet praise given another freely expresses your abundance, vi-
brates and fulfills your destiny as God's servant.

The praise that you allow yourself to receive from another is a
communique of love from the Divine – from one god to another.
Self-abasement, criticism, correction come easily to those who are
in Tradition. They are upheld and supported in your world as a
means of manipulation.

No one needs your condemnation and it cannot serve your purposes. If you wish to alter the actions of another do so by praising what you would have him be. If you could but see the wonderful light that dances around your body as praise is delivered. Everyone delights in the word "good"; everyone recognizes the originating sound of creation.

Even the Lord God can hear your voice lifted up in praise and judges this to be good! Praise, love, joy, prayers, and laughter, these are the only language God speaks. In truth, these are the real communicators on your planet. All else is a lie spoken with the voice of the ego and is superficial. The ego uses its games of attack and defend to divide and separate you from your own essence – to keep you wounded, weakened, and unworthy.

Praise offered to another is always a rendering of what you think and feel about yourself. Each time you are given an opportunity to praise and instead hold your tongue there is a part of you that cries out in anguish. It is this small still part of you that needs more of a voice in your life.

Punish yourself no more for deeds never committed. Deny yourself no more the praise the Creator would have you receive. Praise the sunrise in the morning and never stop until you have praised the stars in the evening sky. By so doing you will be speaking directly to the Divine and your prayers will be heard.

Your praise adds to the structure of love, while every opportunity missed to do so adds to the lies of hate and war. Those who say they cannot make a difference must see that upon their every word hinges the salvation of this world.

Today miss not one glorious opportunity to praise all who come to receive your blessings. See what joy you can give and by so doing you will receive joy. Turn away no one today without looking into their eyes and praising something that is pleasing.

When you begin to look out at the world with a view toward praise, you transform your experience of life and so manifest heaven on earth. Would you withhold heaven from another and deny it to yourself? Offer praise so that all might receive peace.

We who speak would take this opportunity to praise your efforts on our behalf. Although Transformation is never easy, the alternatives are simply unacceptable and so we are eternally grateful for your courage and perseverance. All that is ever asked of you is allowance and willingness. We who love you greatly offer this praise on your behalf, but we do so for it fills us with joy.

# Focus on Remembering
# Who You Are

List all the qualities you have ever thought of as belonging to God. At the beginning of each sentence begin with God is… and then the quality. After you've finished what you consider to be divine attributes then cross out God is and write I AM. Even if you don't believe it, even if the mind denies it, do it anyway. Then place this list somewhere where you can see it everyday.

# Laughter

*"Laughter is the song sung by the soul
radiating out from an expanded heart."*

Laughter is the language of Transformation. Laughter is truly a gift that clears your body of toxins and resistance in order that you might experience a better channel for the Divine connection. Your belief that enlightenment must be difficult and serious work is laughable. How much more pleasurable to create and thus to experience the lightness of a comedy.

But you are horrified – the disasters, the brutality, the evil, the tragedy with which life confronts you. How could we ask that you ignore the suffering surrounding you on every level and literally laugh in the face of constant danger? What danger? Laughter disperses illusion; laugh and it will dissolve before you eyes.

There are certain illusions upon earth that more closely align themselves with universal truth and thus you are more aligned with the Divine while in their performance. Laughter is the song sung by the soul radiating out from an expanded heart.

Huge quantities of healing are released within the being through the magic of laughter. Those who laugh at themselves laugh with God, not in self-abasement but rather from the perspective that what humanity has created is indeed a good joke. To make someone else laugh is a wondrous gift of healing. Many of those who now practice the art of comedy previously practiced the art of medicine. These comedians on your planet shall be called practitioners to the soul throughout the cosmos.

There is more value than merely the strengthening of the immune systems within the body that comes from laughter. There is simultaneously an extraordinary occurrence while in the midst of laughter or when you are able to see humor in a situation.

God does not know His children experience fear, have doubt, cause war, kill and hate one another. So what seems so serious to you is unknown to God. Yet these actions do have consequences, for while you are in their doing you are no longer aligned with the vibration of truth, love and understanding – all that God is.

This is why the bottisatvas (those who sit and wait) or guardian angels are needed as intermediaries between serious man and loving God. We who are in spirit are needed to bridge a gap so large it has served to separate you from your own divinity. But this gulf can be closed with one laugh in an instant in time. Simply laugh at your own consternation and you will be released.

Laughter, humor, praise, and joy allow you to communicate in God's language. Think of it as a different variation in pitch that extends to the ascended realms. Laughter is the accompanying music to the only lyrics the soul can understand – the word good.

The word good shall stand through all eternity as the sound and the song shall be heard in the voice of laughter. It is through this song that you are able to reach and communicate with an ancient but most satisfying part of yourself, for before there was speech as you know it, there was laughter. Our job would be made much easier if there were more laughter to lighten the hearts of the adepts who walk with heavy steps upon their chosen path.

Please remember when we administered a teaching on the molecular structure of hate and then the one of love. In the composition of hate there were many separate and serious segments that attached themselves to the main formation. Each time you laugh, parts of those hate components are dissolved AND at the same time the molecular make up of love increases from within.

Pure laughter is the only pattern that will both feed love and disengage hate. Those of you who believe that you must look upon the horrors in the world and react with horror, or look upon war and attack the warriors, or look upon starvation and deprive self, or look upon disease and become ill at ease – we will tell you that your negativity aids them in their destruction.

Know this: that though these actions be serious, the way out of them is through humor. Darkness is always fed by fear, distrust, deprivation, hate. In truth when you despise a situation you are assisting it through your thoughts. You can never dispel shadows by withholding the light, for shadows are not real and dissolve in light.

Through your free will you have all been given the power to create and sustain the darkness, but you can also extinguish it with the light you hold within yourselves. The light is light in its weight; humor is called levity and it will levitate that which comes before it. Serious things are substantial, weighty, heavy, burdensome.

Go today and laugh at your problems and see if they do not instantly lighten up – for truly you have shined the light of laughter and dismantled part of their molecular structure.

Quite literally they are no longer so intense.

Student of the light, we have always enjoyed your good humor and sense of timing. Go today and lighten the burdens of the world with the power of a laugh.

# *Focus on Laughter*

Laughter is the quickest way to illumination. Whatever lightens your load or brings lightness into your life should be pursued. Humor has a way of harmonizing what is discordant.

Laughter should be a natural reflex in your life like blinking your eyes, breathing and swallowing. You do not need a reason to laugh. There does not need to be anything "funny" in order to initiate laughter. If we learn to laugh more easily and often, more things would seem to be funny. Laugh first and the fun will follow.

Certainly there is no problem or difficulty in our lives that cannot be lightened by a little bit of levity. Perhaps the smile on the Buddha's face is an indication of how we should respond to more situations in life.

For five minutes each day this week, laugh. Your laughter will at first sound false, but if you simply continue to practice you will find true humor in what you are doing. At the end of seven days you will begin to have a natural smile on your face and more humor in your life.

1.  Set a timer for five minutes.

2.  Begin by saying, " HA, HA, HA, HA, HO, HO, HO, HEE, HEE, HEE." Repeat these sounds over and over for the next five minutes in any order you like.

3.  Continue to laugh whether you feel like it or not. Continue to laugh whether you feel stupid or not. Continue to laugh whether it seems funny or not. Do not stop laughing until the full five minutes are up.

Feel the power and perspective that humor can bring into your life. Remember to view humor as an essential part of expanded consciousness and that it is your choice to allow more of it into your life.

313 770 7977

"more-for-you" campaign

$39/Month  MARIA

250 = $350
        39

WEBSITE 389.00
        29.00
       418.00

        39
       37 1
      418.00

# Gratitude and Service

*"Our words are devoid of meaning if you
are unable to access within your divine
memories the truth of who you are.
Express your gratitude for the value each
of you holds for another within the mind
of God."*

Gratitude fortifies your vibration and increases your light aura so that the gifts you deserve might find their way back to you. The magnetism of gratitude is highly contagious. When you walk with gratitude in your being, you become irresistible. Others cannot help but be drawn into your radiant light body that extends outward and penetrates all things.

Creativity is the highest energy found upon this planet, yet gratitude shall be the unifying force field from which all things are drawn together. Gratitude is the only appropriate response for those who remember who they are. Gratitude is the glue that helps you to remember yourself.

Gratitude shall also serve as your guide, showing you when to move out of Tradition. Your feeling of gratitude is the response within the heart as your spirit drinks in the available light found within each new experience. We have explained during these teachings that each experience contains light for the soul. While your spirit consumes the available light within the experience a sense of satisfaction is then translated into a feeling of gratitude.

When you no longer experience gratitude for what you have in your life, for the experiences in your day, or for those who have delivered them to you, then it is time to move. To transit. This we promise – you shall always experience the quality of gratitude while you are present within Transformation. To stay within the essence of Transformation, simply follow the gratitude in your heart that leads to your own creative flow and delivers you out of Tradition.

You have been on a journey through these pages of such magnitude that your mind may attempt to deny your rite of passage. Never doubt that this trip has transformed you forever. Yet know that its ultimate destination leads you back to a place you never left. Transformation is only a one-way trip back into your native state. That state is found in peace of mind.

Your peace of mind does not exist in the illusion of security held by the traditional world. There is no light left in Tradition. No longer look for your peace in the darkness of the world. You could not lose what you are, though you have been given the will to deny it freely.

Transition was given to you as a vehicle that might move you into a place of stillness where you might restore yourself and recognize that you have always had what you need. Transformation is the natural flow of being delivered back to a place you never truly left.

We have seen the vision for this planet. What is to come you shall be grateful for. It is a return to the peace of God, to the paradisiacal state of being. Nothing less is possible. Its delivery is dependent upon the courage of those souls who have agreed to return through the restoration of a vision.

There was a vision perfected in the mind of God that was to be given to this planet. This vision set forth truth and mirrored the wholeness of the Divine. The vision shattered, separated, and then fell to earth to be reassembled. Each of you is a fragment of that dream God sent to this plane. You are not an accident; you are the purposeful peace in Divine mind and you are on a miraculous mission.

Within your imagination lives the vision with which you were entrusted. It is time to awaken the dreamers so that they might together remember their parts and realize their dream. It is time that personalities be put aside in favor of the real purpose for re-incarnating.

Do not listen to the mind that will insist this is arrogance. Instead know that it is arrogant to deny your part in the restoration of sanity. No longer disregard God by bowing to the mind. To believe that you are anything less than an apostle of peace keeps you from experiencing the message you came to deliver.

This message we bring is not for all. Transformation of your planet is merely a return to what has always existed as the Divine dream. What you have created on this plane is a nightmare. It is time for the dreamers to awaken from the fantasy of perception into the reality of love. This process of restoration is not difficult so do not allow the mind to become discouraged. Your efforts at this time shall serve 10,000-fold. The high vibration called forth by the few shall prevail and so establish the resulting order for the many.

The new mathematical progression on earth shall be concerned with the unity found in the whole. There need be only one in order to reinstate the peace within the whole – one whole essential energy, living a creative life in gratitude, serving as a signal that will awaken others.

Not all those on earth feel their vibration sufficiently to restore 10,000, and so many upon your plane are now choosing through physical death to return to a formless state of harmlessness.

The egos of those who deny through their life style the very purpose of living shall now simply pass into spirit and so aid the

199

planet through their own expanded revelation – that all life is impeccable, positive, evolving energy that is constantly transforming. Those who remove themselves physically at this time shall remain with the earth in order to assist spiritually in her efforts toward Transformation.

No longer allow your mind to tell you what you do is unimportant. You are vital and essential to the plan as it is unfolding upon your planet. No one is more so than another, yet each who is willing to listen shall become a living link in a chain that may never again be broken, forged forever out of the spirit of love. Through this eternal chain shall now pass the peace for which you long.

The life you are living here shall form the very foundation of the lives you are to live elsewhere. Every act is significant, yet failure is impossible for you are asked only to remember what can never be forgotten and each experience upon your path leads you back to where you belong.

The Cycle of Ascendancy has assisted in restoring the process of memory. The cycle itself is unending though our teaching be finished. Success is guaranteed for it is natural to move toward unity, to move toward light, to move toward love. You are simply remembering yourself now through your divine memory, so that you might recall who you have always been.

Each who hears this message stands as an Initiator for 10,000 who are with you in spirit. You are used as a crystal, magnifying the frequency of the messages of the Divine.

Each action taken, each word spoken, each thought generated adds to or detracts from another's ability to awaken.

Not all must physically be expressing in order to transform this planet. You stand in substance for those spirits whose conscious minds would otherwise interfere with their abilities to reclaim the truth. When you stir you cause movement to occur in another through your light vibration that has the potential to awaken all.

200

You are asked to trust in this regard, for you cannot always see the effects of your works with the physical eyes. Never doubt, however, the power of the unseen, for it is awesome

Through the unifying force of gratitude a handful may elevate the earth. This was done before with only twelve. You know not what you do, but there shall come a time when the souls of millions will acknowledge your contribution to their evolvement and you will clearly see the part you played in the process of peace.

Our words are devoid of meaning if you are unable to access within your own divine memories the truth of which we speak. Express your gratitude for the value each of you holds for another.

Perhaps your mind refuses the responsibility for another's ascension. To this we say that every living thing is responsible for every other living thing. We who have evolved so completely that the lowered vibration of form is difficult, are still dependent upon your ascension for our further progress. We are responsible for you, you are responsible for them, they are responsible to others.

Yet only one, only you, needs to remember in order for the world to become restored. Without you this vision will perish. Without you, we cannot ascend, for without you we are incomplete.

There is only the One who has fragmented and now attempts to remember itself through the union of all. There is no one else out there but you. We beg you to awaken now and witness the plan God has for us all. No one may leave without themselves; it is folly to think that you may progress while abandoning yourself. No one is lost when you are found. Failure is impossible, for the cause from which you were created has always been won and will always be One.

Each of you has assisted in the transformation of another, each has healed another's heart, each has supported another's vision. Each of you has cradled and lifted another.

Each has ascended high ground and will bring back within them a new vision, a signal to the soul that the Son within has risen and with it a new dawn of consciousness. Traveling the Cycle of Ascendancy on these pages has moved you closer together and so closer to your own knowingness.

You need not be perfect to perform this service for self and for another, you need only be grateful for the opportunities to serve as they are presented. Serve one another, serve the group, serve the planet. Service is foreign to many. Understand that the only way to serve self is to assist another, the only way to serve another is to fulfill the self.

Do not misconstrue "good works" for service. "Good works" are moral judgments made by the mind on behalf of one deemed to be inferior and in need. They serve no one and further confuse the energy of your plane. You are the sole proprietor of your life, yet to know self you must be of use. To be of use is to be in service.

You have been filled by these teachings and they have awakened within you a reunion of spirit. It is time now to release into the outer world, time to spill over in gratitude, sharing, and service.

Though another does not need what you have, it is vital that you receive the opportunity to give to yourself through another. In this way do you demonstrate to the doubtful mind that the most direct route for receiving is through the giving.

Since beauty, truth, joy, and love lie within, it is important for Transformation that they be expressed outwardly so that you might share your experience with the world. This is the need now upon your plane.

You have come to manifest divine mind in matter. The natural order is always from spirit to substance. God is the eternal Source, the one divine flame of pure intense light.

You are a brilliant spark that has jumped from that eternal flame to bring light into a world of darkness. It is time to share the light that you have found within yourself.

You need to give your blessing to another so that you might truly receive it. We who are in service to humanity ask that you join us, expand yourself so that you might fulfill your destiny and we might all ascend through service to one another.

We began this Unbound series of teachings with a lesson on words. Now the time has come to continue your communication to each light holder without them. Listen to the master within and write your own ending to this chapter that in truth began before time.

We have saved something for you. Listen to us who will soon speak to you with no words, but rather through the connection of the heart that unites us all – one heart beating the universal rhythm of the peace of God. If you listen to the heart's desire you will be able to decipher your own vision and see it come true.

Each will receive differently – some will see, some will hear, some will write, some will draw. What you share with yourself now, shall be a service to all creation.

In these UNBOUND teachings, you have had the opportunity to become more unlimited, more unqualified, more unrestricted. You have become a disciple of your own inner wisdom, reunited with the master within.

The end of these words is near, for they can never deliver you into the realm of the imagination. Words may only activate your intuitive voice so that you might listen to a higher frequency. It is the sound heard in silence, it is the sight seen without eyes – these are the tools to use for new awareness.

The true language of the soul is spoken with symbols. Truth for the heart is garbed in the robes of myth and legend. It is through the imagination that two thousand years of peace will be delivered to the planet. We ask that you write your dream for earth, that you travel into the recesses of your being and discover the part that you are to play in her tale.

Reality mirrors imagination. Allow the fantasy to be as grand as its creator might invent, knowing that you call forth from the ethers what you will have happen. If you can perceive divine reality, it is possible for you to live your life in harmony with who you are – this is your birthright, this is your spirit Unbound.

## Your Legend

Once upon a time, in a not
too distant land, there lived an
angelic spirit who came to earth disguised
as a mortal called __OBIDIKE AL-KAMAU__
__LACY B. CHIMNEY Jr.__ .
(your name)
This beloved being was sent
to fulfill a divine mission...

finish the story
for you are the Author of
your life

## About the Author

Dorien Israel is a happy, healthy, wholly alive woman who has aligned her life with her highest values and is joyously sharing the dream of simplicity and self sufficiency with others. Dorien teaches dance, yoga, qi gong, meditation, and is a reiki master. She spends four month of the year in the U.S.A. and the remainder on the tropical island of Koh Samui Thailand where she offers unique retreats focusing on the discovery of "who you truly are".

Dorien is the author of two other books; **Tao Passages**, and **The Way To The One I Am**.

You can contact Dorien at her website:
**www. BecomingUnbound. com**

CPSIA information can be obtained
at www.ICGtesting.com
Printed in the USA
LVHW031309271220
675115LV00042B/1083

9 781412 061308